HIDDEN WITHIN

HIDDEN WITHIN

THE 40-DAY SCRIPTURE MEMORY PROJECT

Jason S. Lancaster

CrossLink Publishing

CrossLink Publishing
1601 Mt. Rushmore Rd, STE 3288
Rapid City, SD 57702

Ordering Information:
Quantity sales. Special discounts are available on quantity purchases by corporations, associations, and others. For details, contact the "Special Sales Department" at the address above.

Hidden Within/Lancaster —1st ed.

ISBN 978-1-63357-183-9

Library of Congress Control Number: 2019945948

First edition: 10 9 8 7 6 5 4 3 2 1

What Others Are Saying

"*Hidden Within* impacted me in very tangible ways during a stressful time in my life. I can remember lying in bed, struggling to sleep as anxious thoughts filled my head, and then opening *Hidden Within* and walking through the verses I had memorized and allowing the Spirit to remind me of His truth. Scripture memorization is vital to actively remembering and living God's truth, and *Hidden Within* is a great tool for doing it!"
—David Chookaszian, senior business development executive

"Pastor Jason's ministry taught me to love, appreciate, and utilize the Scriptures in a new way, and *Hidden Within* was an invaluable tool that equipped me to share my faith with my teammates. Having the Word of God on my heart and as the foundation of my thoughts has brought me closer to God and enabled me to better fulfill the Great Commission. I'm so thankful for *Hidden Within* because I know that it will help anyone drink deeply from God's Word!"
—Tommy Doles, Northwestern University football player, 2014–2018

"There was a time in my life when I was battling some sinful patterns and deep sadness as a result. Pastor Jason's modeling and tools for Scripture memory had a significant impact on my life during that time. God's Word was breath in my lungs and my orientation toward right thinking. Hiding God's Word in my heart has helped me to think rightly about Him, myself, and others."
—Laila Bechtle, special education teacher

"The *Hidden Within* devotionals and memory verses have been so ON POINT for us—so providential."
—Danielle and Conner Ray, musicians

"Pastor Jason Lancaster's passion for God's Word was evident in exemplifying Scripture memorization and consistently teaching and encouraging the Church to make Scripture memory a significant spiritual discipline. *Hidden Within* was a creative way for Jason to bring us on board with a daily devotional and a systematic process for memorizing verses. I confess to being a poor memorizer, yet I was able to gather multiple Scripture verses through this process, which has enriched my spiritual journey."
—Tom Hartman, business development executive

"As our pastor, Jason modeled Scripture memory from the pulpit, which inspired us to try his method. *Hidden Within* was an easy way to memorize Scripture and enabled us to recall God's Word as we faced life's challenges. Being able to dwell on the truths of Scripture at any moment continues to be a blessing in our lives."
—Matt and Laura Wright, IT specialist and high school English teacher

"The people in Jason Lancaster's church and sphere of life have benefited eternally from his passion for hiding God's Word in his heart because he uses that hidden Word to intercede for us. So, I wholeheartedly recommend *Hidden Within*."
—Sheri Scalero, Bible study leader

"I have had occasion to memorize substantial amounts of God's Word, and I have to say that, of anything that I have done, it has had the greatest impact on my spiritual growth. *Hidden Within* provides a simple, straightforward method that makes memorization possible, and by which anyone who wants to, can do it.

Verses are organized topically, and brief devotionals are included that aid understanding and practical application. I wholeheartedly endorse *Hidden Within*."
—Norman P. Blair, MD, FARVO, professor of ophthalmology, University of Illinois College of Medicine

"When it comes to Scripture memory, Jason practices what he preaches. He not only exhorted the congregation to memorize Scripture, but he set an example by doing it himself. In *Hidden Within*, Jason provides a list of verses organized by topic with daily lessons. After completing the forty days, I found myself missing the lessons and wishing there were more."
—Karin Richards, homeschool mom

"*Hidden Within* was designed with a shepherd's heart. It both practically helps believers build a consistent rhythm of Scripture memory into their lives and builds them up in the faith, encouraging them to see the end goal of Scripture memory: a deeper relationship with the Lord."
—Kyle Butson, financial consultant

"Scripture memory is such an important way to internalize the Word of God. As a pastor, Jason encouraged us not just to empty our hearts of idolatry and worry, but to FILL our heart with the Word. He emphasized Scripture memorization and gave personal examples of its impact. *Hidden Within* is a great tool that anyone can use to start memorizing Scripture—it works because it is simple! I used it as part of my daily devotional and was amazed at how much Scripture I was able to memorize in a short time."
—Ben Mangrich, elder at Evanston Bible Fellowship

"*Hidden Within* not only taught me the value of Scripture memory, but it was also a practical tool that helped me store God's

Word in my heart in a lasting way. Now, I have authoritative, infallible verses in the depths of my soul to encourage, convict, and remind me of the deep love of Jesus."
—Danny Russell, pastoral resident

Contents

The Word

Love

Witness

Compassion

The Church

The Future

Glory

Acknowledgments

I wish to express many thanks to those who have influenced and encouraged the publication of *Hidden Within*.

To my brothers and sisters from Providence Church, Evanston Bible Fellowship, and Village Bible Church, where we joyfully spurred one another to get in the Word and get the Word in us.

To Danny Russell and Kyle Butson, for their early encouragement and vision to get the thrust of *Hidden Within* just right.

To Fran Taylor, for her outstanding editing skills, clever insights, and wise suggestions.

To Andy Uyeda, for working hard to create the *Hidden Within* app so that the memory method can be electronically assessible.

To Kelly Rochleau, for creating the fresh artwork for the book and the app.

To Elwood Hale, for counseling me during a difficult season and spurring me on with an attainable method of Scripture memorization to last a lifetime.

To my wife and kids, who encourage me to press on in the Word and will of God.

Introduction

My Desperation

I was approaching thirty, and life wasn't working out the way I hoped. I was serving at a dying church, and I would eventually be its last pastor. It was my first church out of seminary, and at the age of twenty-five, I was just grateful for an opportunity to preach. I was naïve. Many of the individuals were earnest Christians, but we were dysfunctional together. As the pastor, I took many hits and constantly faced a mountain of criticism. My mantra during this time was, "I just don't know what to do." I tried everything: bold evangelism, forty days of fasting, countless hours of prayer, expository preaching, leadership training, and intentional discipleship. The harder I pushed, the more difficult the situation seemed to become, and the deeper my despair grew.

My personal life was a mess, as well. My wife struggled with postpartum depression, and I was playing the part of the dutiful, yet checked-out husband. We had two young children—just thirteen months apart—who had a variety of needs. Our support structure was minimal, as we were several states away from family and close friends. We were hanging on by a thread. For years, I kept a daily journal, which included a variety of prayers and petitions for my family, the church, and myself. However, I completely stopped journaling as the prayers turned sad and depressing.

Life's demands seemed nonstop and crushing. On top of pastoral duties, I had to work a part-time job to meet our financial needs. After work, I helped with our children, which might include waking up a few times in the middle of the night. The cleaning and grocery shopping duties also fell to me during this season. During one grocery trip, I remember just staring at the items on the shelf in a daze. The shelves blurred before me as I daydreamed about having another life. Demands and disappointments overwhelmed me, and I wanted out.

Different temptations sought me out for temporary relief. I thought about turning to idols, like sexual immorality or greed, but the Lord had redeemed me from that empty way of life. So, I stayed away from the sins of my past but started dabbling with new sins, such as bitterness and resentfulness. This dual threat was ripping me apart from the inside. No matter what I did, I couldn't stop the looping thoughts that kept returning to bitterness and resentfulness. The church was not supposed to be like this. Family was not supposed to be like this. Life was not supposed to be like this.

I'd like to think I was still trying to walk with the Lord during this time. I kept crying out to God as I daily prayed and stayed in His Word. I kept up my pastoral duties of preaching, evangelism, and discipleship. But I was low and simply wanted out of this life and to be in God's presence.

The breaking point came when I started thinking of different ways to take my own life. Before this time, I had never had suicidal thoughts, but my mind was suddenly overrun. My thoughts were out of control, and I couldn't rein them in through prayer, Bible study, or even preaching. I just wanted to leave this earth altogether.

Your Desperation

Over the years, I have encountered many people who were broken and hopeless. Simply asking how they were doing would produce instant tears. From the woman whose husband had destroyed the family, to the man whose pride upended his life, to the young collegiate drowning in loneliness, the details of the stories change from person to person, but the overarching theme of desperation stays the same: When life's troubles attack, the soul begins to buckle.

You may be there right now. A tragedy has struck, and it has knocked the light out within. All is dark. The loss of a life, the loss of a job, or the loss of a relationship may have sent you spiraling downward. When will the darkness lift? When will the clouds break?

The daily grind of life may be ripping you apart. Busyness, combined with unrelenting demands, can lead to an emotional crash. Life seems doable as you crank out unreasonable hours at work, school, or home until one more thing is added. What's the big deal about working a couple of weekends per month? Or writing an extra paper for school? Or caring for your sick or aging parent for a couple of nights? If life weren't already crushing you, these would be a breeze. However, the added pace can wear on your soul.

Visions, dreams, and goals help keep humans moving forward. Yet, you can't seem to kick the thoughts of your disappointments. You expected your career to take off, but now you are relegated to a job filled with monotony. Your retirement years were supposed to be a great reward for years of hard work, but the physical and emotional pain is more than you expected. Your relationships were supposed to bring you joy, but instead, they have left you disappointed and confused. Your zeal, energy, and drive are gone and have been replaced with one big sense of "blah."

Like me, you may be beyond the point of giving up. You are numbly moving through life. You are desperate and your soul is clinging to the dust. You cannot go any lower.

Hope

As my life broke, I was desperate for rescue. A man in my church recommended I go see an older gentleman who spent his time counseling people out of his house. God used this man, Elwood Hale, to literally save my life. Through discussion, prayer, and interaction with the Bible, we worked through a variety of my heart issues. It's amazing how counseling done with the appropriate mixture of compassion and confrontation can alter a life. To have another draw out your emotions, expectations, pains, and sins can be eye-opening.

It's not just about gushing disappointments but finding encouragement in the gospel of Jesus Christ, who changes people by His Spirit, His Church, and His Word. By the power of the indwelling Holy Spirit, no one has to stay stuck in hopelessness. Through the encouragement of God's people in the Church, we can press on through the darkness. And the replenishing and reordering effects of His Word can renew our minds.

It was this renewal of mind that I needed. I had a lot of messed-up thoughts. Elwood told me I needed to replace my skewed thinking with God's Word through Scripture memorization. He believed the more God's Word was dominating my thoughts, the less consumed I would be with resentfulness, bitterness, and despair. My experience memorizing Scripture had been minimal, but I was desperate. The deep immersion of Scripture memory would be a new weapon to penetrate the darkness, dislodge unwanted thoughts, and replace them with the Word of God.

Method

Elwood gave me a simple method to consistently memorize Scripture. It was a method that began by taking five to ten minutes each day, and over the years it has led to memorizing hundreds of verses. This is not a boast in my ability, but in my desperation for God's Word. Over the years, I have branched out to memorize larger portions of Scripture for my personal edification. In addition, I have had the privilege of reciting these to my congregation for their encouragement. The story of my desperation has led others to pursue Scripture memorization so that God's Word can be a light to them, as well.

There are many methods of Scripture memorization that have helped people hide God's Word in their hearts. The method in this book is not my invention, nor am I advocating it is better than other methods. It's just the method that was passed on to me by Elwood, and I have found it very helpful. In addition, it's extremely easy! The aim is to memorize over ten verses in a forty-day period. Each passage will fall under a major topic, such as heart, gospel, love, glory, etc. These topics will last four days in length, and each day will have a special devotional written out of my interactions with the Word. The daily memory work will follow the devotion and need to be repeated as many times as indicated. Each verse will need to be written on a 3x5 notecard, so gather ten notecards for the duration. If you are a high achiever, get a metal ring to hold them together. If you have a smart device, feel free to do the Scripture memory on the *Hidden Within* App. You can download it on iTunes or Google Play, and record your memory work through the app.

Motivation

I hope these daily devotionals will motivate and encourage you to memorize the Word of God. God uses many means of grace to strengthen His people. The local church is the main community where believers empower one another to love God and others. In addition, the reading and preaching of God's Word, prayer, and obeying the commands of God are all means for our growth. But there is something about hiding God's Word in the heart that infuses all of life with God-centered thinking, especially during times of suffering. I'm hoping to walk with you and lead you to hide God's comforting Word in your heart over the next forty days.

The Heart

Proverbs 4:23

Keep your heart with all vigilance,
for from it flow the springs of life.

Day 1: The Heart

If a college student is interested in dating a certain person, he or she might be given the advice, "Guard your heart." What is meant by this phrase, "guard your heart," is that you shouldn't get emotionally involved in a relationship too quickly, but you should wait and see if there is godly compatibility and whether or not the feelings are mutual. But if someone forges ahead with an unguarded heart, he or she risks rejection or becoming trapped in a dysfunctional relationship. With the dire consequences in view, this sage advice continues from one campus to the next.

Perhaps that could be a tiny application of biblical wisdom, but the original verse branches out to include all of life. Proverbs 4:23 (NIV) says:

> Above all else, guard your heart, for it is
> the wellspring of life.

When the Bible talks about your heart, it refers to the core of who you are. It's your thoughts, your motives, your emotions, your personality, and the spiritual part of your makeup. Proverbs 27:19 (ESV) puts it like this:

> As in water face reflects face, so the heart
> of man reflects the man.

When we talk about getting to know someone better, we mean that we are getting to know their heart and who they really are.

Why guard your heart? Why the urgency to do this "above all else"? Because out of your heart comes your character, which is revealed in your choices, your speech, and your actions. Just as a "wellspring" is the source of a stream or a river, so the heart is the source of your life. From the heart springs forth the core of who you are. The reason you want to guard your heart is that you want to guard your life.

To guard your heart means to protect what comes in and goes out. You must constantly be on guard and keep your heart with all vigilance because it's the command center for all your words and actions. The Puritan writer John Flavel used the example of guarding your heart akin to a besieged garrison with enemies on the outside and treacherous citizens on the inside. The imagery is dated, but the idea is good, so let me run with it in a modern equivalent.

Before I was a Christian, I had an unguarded and rebellious heart. My heart was like a frat house that partied hard. I had no restraints on the anger and foul language that came out and that I let in. I had no guard on the amount of immorality that I expressed and invited in. Greed came out of my heart and freely welcomed new greedy ideas. Anxiety needed no key to come and go as it pleased. There was freedom for sin to rush out of my corrupt heart and come in to corrupt it even more. Then Jesus demolished and removed my frat-house heart and gave me a new "White House" heart. I moved from an anything-goes frat house to a heavily guarded White House (one of the most guarded homes in the country).

If you are a believer, your heart is now purified and the Holy Spirit lives in you and enables you to guard your heart. By God's grace, you can now be vigilant in guarding what comes in and goes out of your heart. To that end, a crucial weapon in guarding your heart is Scripture memorization. As you freely welcome in the Word of God and store it deep in your core so that it impacts your thoughts, emotions, plans, and words, eventually and powerfully it will gush forth into a life lived for the glory of God.

Memory Work

- Write out Proverbs 4:23 along with the reference on the front of a 3x5 card. Or, download the app, Hidden Within.
- Write just the reference on the back of the card (Proverbs 4:23).
- Repeat it 25 times and mark the back of the card each time you say it.
- Say the reference before and after you say the verse.
- It's okay to look at the verse, but eventually you will say it without looking.

Day 2: The Heart

What is going on in your heart? Jeremiah 17:9 says:

> The heart is deceitful above all things, and
> desperately sick; who can understand it?

When a Disney movie tells you to trust your heart, just yell out right there in the movie theater, "Don't do it!" Now, for Christians, this desperately sick heart has been removed and a new heart has been put in its place. When we acknowledge our sin, repent, and put our faith in Jesus, we are changed and given a new heart and a new Spirit. Ezekiel 36:26–27 says,

> And I will give you a new heart, and a
> new spirit I will put within you. And I will
> remove the heart of stone from your flesh
> and give you a heart of flesh. And I will
> put my Spirit within you, and cause you to
> walk in my statutes and be careful to obey
> my rules.

> **Though our hearts are no longer enslaved to sin, they still have a propensity to dabble in the old ways of life.**

Before we were Christians, we had hard hearts against God, but now they are new, soft and malleable. Because of this, we want to obey and worship Him. However, deep inside our regenerated hearts, something is still off (call it the "flesh" or indwelling sin). Though our hearts are no longer enslaved to sin, they still have a propensity to dabble in the old ways of life. Our hearts are constantly choosing between good and evil, between wisdom and foolishness, between worshiping God and worshiping idols.

So, I ask again: What is going on in your heart? Maybe you have no clue. A helpful hint to see what's going on in your heart is to pay attention to your words. Your words reveal your heart condition. For example, if your words are foolish and hurt others, you don't have a word problem but a heart problem. Jesus said in Luke 6:45,

> The good person out of the good treasure
> of his heart produces good, and the evil
> person out of his evil treasure produces
> evil, for out of the abundance of the heart
> his mouth speaks.

Pay attention to the words that gush from your heart.

Another helpful hint is to pay attention to your actions because they reveal your heart, as well. Once Jesus spoke about the heart in the context of what defiles a person. Defilement is not a matter of clean or unclean foods, but of the heart. Mark 7:20–23 says:

And he said,

> What comes out of a person is what
> defiles him. For from within, out of the
> heart of man, come evil thoughts, sexual
> immorality, theft, murder, adultery,
> coveting, wickedness, deceit, sensuality,
> envy, slander, pride, foolishness. All these
> evil things come from within, and they
> defile a person.

The heart is the root issue of all these behaviors.

What's going on in your heart? This knowledge starts by owning your sin as *your* sin. Don't blame others or circumstances for your foolish words. Don't explain away your sinful actions by pointing the finger elsewhere, but instead turn it around and point it at your heart. If you fail to repent of your personal sin, you will continue to gush out pain on others and disobedience to God. But if you see that something is wrong and that something is you, then you can receive forgiveness in Jesus and ask the Lord to help you live out your new gospel-transformed heart.

Ultimately, only God knows all that is going on in your heart, so make these words your desperate plea:

> Search me, O God, and know my heart!
> Try me and know my thoughts!
> And see if there be any grievous way in
> me,
> and lead me in the way everlasting!
> (Psalm 139:23–24)

Memory Work

- Repeat 20 times Proverbs 4:23 and mark the back of the card each time you say it.
- Don't forget to say the reference before and after you say the verse.

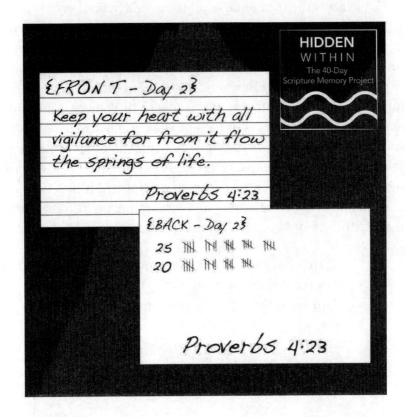

Day 3: The Heart

My wife and I used to watch a TV documentary called NY Med. It's a reality show that reveals the emotions and grind inside a variety of New York City hospitals. Often the storyline surrounded some type of heart surgery. The surgeon would meet with the patient and discuss all the problems with their heart: clots, disease progression, etc. The surgeon would then say, "It looks bad, but I am not going to know how bad until I open you up." This was always a setup, because in the next scene they would open up the patient and it would be worse than they thought. Sometimes the heart had additional problems, other times blood started to squirt out, and sometimes the patient's heart even stopped beating for a while. Eventually, the surgeon came through, the patient lived, and everyone praised and hugged the surgeon.

Let's now do a little heart surgery of sorts where you are the patient. It's not physical heart surgery, but surgery on your unseen heart. You may have a variety of problems and ongoing issues: nagging fears, low-grade depression, unhappiness in your life, distractibility, anger, worry and anxiety, out-of-control debt, lack of motivation, unchecked sexual desires, out-of-control food cravings, a desire for more money or possessions, and countless relational problems. The issues you have most likely stem from a problem in your heart. Would you be willing to let God, the Great Physician, open you up? Perhaps that's scary, because who knows what He will find or what problems will gush out? But God is a tender Physician who loves you. God is also a skilled Physician who knows what's wrong and exactly what needs to be done. You can trust Him and His work on you.

God knows exactly what He will find when you open your heart to Him. He knows you have areas of your life that are contrary to His Word and offensive to His holiness. Yet, He doesn't turn away from you if you come humbly and broken through Jesus. On the cross, Jesus took the punishment for your evil heart. God now speaks words of forgiveness, healing, reconciliation, and restoration. God is not here to condemn but to welcome forgiven sinners and declare them His righteous saints. There is no need to be afraid of what God might find because He already knows. He still loves you and desires that you be healed.

> There is no need to be afraid of what God might find because He already knows.

Many churches sing the song "Here's My Heart" by David Crowder. It's a song in which we ask God to open us up and speak what is true. And the surprise is that He doesn't speak words of judgment but words of grace. May God bring truth and healing to your heart today.

> Here's my heart, Lord, speak what is true. I am found, I am Yours. I am loved, I'm made pure. I have life; I can breathe. I am healed. I am free. Here's my heart, Lord, speak what is true. You are strong, You are sure. You are life, You endure. You are good, always true. You are light breaking through. Here's my heart, Lord, speak what is true. Here's my life, Lord, speak what is true. I am found, I am Yours. I am loved, I'm made pure. I have life; I can breathe. I am healed; I am free. You are strong, You are sure. You are life, You

endure. You are good, always true. You are light breaking through. You are more than enough. You are here; You are love. You are hope; You are grace. You're all I have; You're everything. Here's my heart, Lord, speak what is true.

Memory Work

- Repeat 15 times Proverbs 4:23 and mark the back of the card each time you say it.
- Don't forget to say the reference before and after you say the verse.

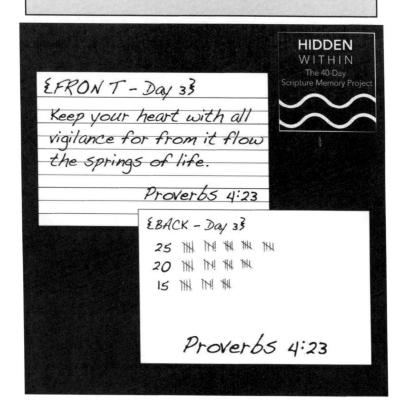

Day 4: The Heart

Are you convinced that your heart can't refuse sin and know joy until your circumstances change? You may confess sin, ask God to search your heart, and speak what is true, but you are not so sure it's going to do any good because the pain is too overwhelming. Yet, the Bible reveals there is a certain heart that can endure the hard times. Proverbs 17:22 is a demonstration of this type of heart:

> A joyful heart is good medicine, but a
> crushed spirit dries up the bones.

A person with a *crushed spirit* has lost the will to carry on. A crushed spirit can take you out faster than a crushed body. Hopeless despair has settled in, and you feel like there will be no joy ever again. Many of you have faced or are facing the debilitating effects of despair. You are crushed in spirit and can't go on. It's like you are wasting away.

The flipside of a crushed spirit is a heart full of joy. It's this heart that is "good medicine" no matter the circumstances. Think about the apostle Paul and Silas, beaten and locked in prison, and yet they were singing hymns to God (Acts 16:25). How is that even possible? Their joy was not circumstantial. We often think we would be happier if God just flipped the circumstances. Yet, it looks like we can have deep-seated joy in God no matter the pain. First Thessalonians 5:16 says, "Be joyful always" (NIV). That's what we want, but how do we get and sustain such joy?

It all comes back to the heart. You need to know deep inside that God is with you in your suffering. God knows your anguished state, and He will never leave you nor forsake you. You can't point the finger at God and say, "You are up there while I'm down here suffering. You don't understand." You can't say that because Jesus entered into the fullness of our humanity. Jesus was deeply in touch with the brokenness of the world and was called a "man of sorrows." Isaiah 53:3–4 says:

> He was despised and rejected by men; a man of sorrows and acquainted with grief; and as one from whom men hide their faces he was despised, and we esteemed him not.

> Surely he has borne our griefs and carried our sorrows; yet we esteemed him stricken, smitten by God, and afflicted.

Jesus bore the full extent of a broken world by suffering in His body on the cross for your sin. You contributed to His sorrows and sufferings because of your sin. To top it all off, He felt the sorrow of the cross as the Father turned His face away and poured out His wrath because of your sin. Yet, the One who was punished by the wrath of God in your place for your sin is also the one moved with compassion for you.

The Bible even speaks of Jesus' sympathizing with you in your weakness. Hebrews 4:15–16 says:

> For we do not have a high priest who is unable to sympathize with our weaknesses, but one who in every respect has been tempted as we are, yet without sin. Let us then with confidence draw near to the throne of grace, that we may receive mercy and find grace to help in time of need.

As you suffer from sin, temptations, and strong emotions, Jesus can sympathize with you. Though He never sinned or was ruled by strong emotions, He can sympathize with you because He knows what you are going through. As you suffer, He not only sympathizes with you but gives you mercy and grace as you cry out to Him in your time of need. You can be emotionally honest before God (He's not surprised) and receive mercy and grace.

> Let us then with confidence draw near to the throne of grace

Receiving God's grace and mercy doesn't cause you to be a chipper, constantly smiling Christian who brushes off the suffering of life. But it does produce a deep-seated joy in the Lord that can be *good medicine* regardless of the circumstances.

Memory Work

- Repeat 10 times Proverbs 4:23 and mark the back of the card each time you say it.
- Don't forget to say the reference before and after you say the verse.

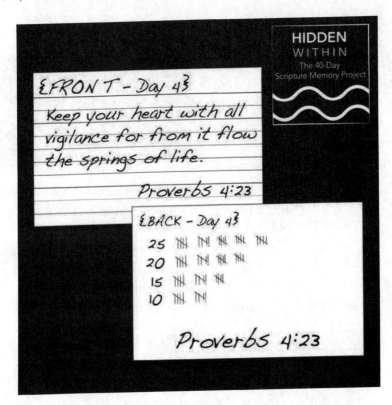

The Gospel

1 Corinthians 15:3-4

For I delivered to you as of first importance what I also received: that Christ died for our sins in accordance with the Scriptures, that he was buried, that he was raised on the third day in accordance with the Scriptures.

Day 5: The Gospel

The gospel is the good news of what God has done in Christ to rescue lost humanity from their sins and adopt them as children of God. A good summary of the gospel comes from 1 Corinthians 15:3–4:

> For I delivered to you as of first
> importance what I also received: that
> Christ died for our sins in accordance
> with the Scriptures, that he was buried,
> that he was raised on the third day in
> accordance with the Scriptures.

This is the core of the gospel and the good news that Christians believe and proclaim. Jesus Christ was the sinless One who died in place of sinners. On the cross, He bore the penalty and the full force of the wrath of God for sinners. He was buried and remained dead until the third day when He rose again. The Father accepted His perfect sacrifice, death was defeated, and Satan was crushed. Now, through faith in Jesus Christ, repentant sinners are forgiven and adopted into the family of God.

This gospel is not a new idea on God's part but played out "in accordance with the Scriptures." There are a variety of historical, scriptural prophecies that looked ahead to the work of Jesus Christ. Take, for example, Isaiah 53:5–6:

> But he was pierced for our transgressions,
> he was crushed for our iniquities;
> the punishment that brought us peace
> was on him,

and by his wounds we are healed.

We all, like sheep, have gone astray,
each of us has turned to our own way;
and the Lord has laid on him
the iniquity of us all.

God's wrath coming upon the Suffering Servant in place of sinners was prophesied in the Old Testament. Now, the gospel of Jesus is proclaiming the fulfillment of the suffering Servant dying on the cross for sinners to be healed.

This is the gospel offered to the whole world, but it hits home by faith and explodes in the heart of one forgiven and adopted by God. This explosion of the gospel happened in my life at the age of nineteen. I was a punk kid living my own life apart from God. The trajectory of my life was headed to hell, as I was steeped in immorality, greed, and foul language. Religion masqueraded in my life with traditional church attendance and a variety of spiritual symbols on my walls and around my neck. But it was a mockery, as my lifestyle betrayed the truth of the gospel of God in the work of Christ. My phoniness even passed a Christian screening, as I was hired by one of the best Christian camps in the nation. At camp, I was supposed to be leading kids to Christ, but instead the Lord brought me to Himself. I heard the gospel and was so convicted over my sin that I broke down in sobs, repented, and turned to God for forgiveness in Jesus. The gospel of Jesus invaded my life, and I was saved and adopted into the family of God.

God's gospel—prophesied according to the Scriptures and fulfilled in Jesus—has invaded your life, as well. You have a salvation story. It might not be dramatic, but it is just as valuable. Pause for a moment and flash back to God's intervention in your life to bring you to Jesus. Recall your specific rebellion against God and His gospel pursuit. Your new memory verse captures the historical work of Christ on your behalf. As you meditate on the gospel, may you rejoice in God's intervention in your life to forgive your sins and bring you into His family forever.

Memory Work

- Write out 1 Corinthians 15:3-4 along with the reference on the front of a 3x5 card. Or download the app, *Hidden Within*.
- Write just the reference on the back of the card (1 Corinthians 15:3–4).
- Repeat it 25 times and mark the back of the card each time you say it.
- Say the reference before and after you say the verse.
- Return to the Proverbs 4:23 card.
- Repeat it once and mark the back of the card.

{FRONT - Day 5}

For I delivered to you as of first importance what I also received; that Christ died for our sins in accordance with the scriptures, that he was buried, that he was raised on the third day in accordance with the scriptures.

I Corinthians 15:3-4

{BACK - Day 5}

25 卌 卌 卌 卌 卌

I Corinthians 15:3-4

HIDDEN WITHIN
The 40-Day
Scripture Memory Project

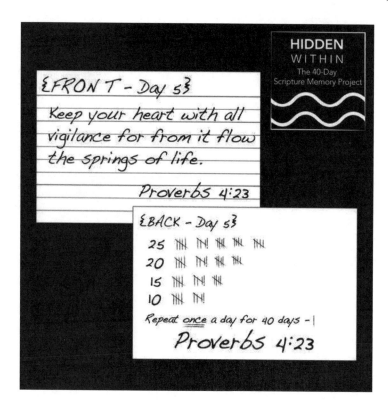

Day 6: The Gospel

Once, there was a big storm in the area where we lived. Heavy winds came through the neighborhood, ripping trees to shreds. Branches were down, and leaves were everywhere. As my wife and I walked around the neighborhood afterward to survey the damage, we saw one tree completely uprooted. Other trees in the area were devastated, with leaves stripped and branches broken off, but they were still standing. For the uprooted tree, life was over, and the next day, it was cut into firewood. Similarly, storms of life will come to break and attempt to uproot you. However, if you are rooted deep in the gospel of God, you will be battered, but not uprooted.

. . . if you are rooted deep in the gospel of God, you will be battered, but not uprooted.

The apostle Paul was a man rooted deep in the gospel of God and was able to withstand a variety of storms. His passion for the gospel seeps through in Romans 1:1–4:

> Paul, a servant of Christ Jesus, called to be an apostle, set apart for the gospel of God, which he promised beforehand through his prophets in the holy Scriptures, concerning his Son, who was descended from David according to the flesh and was declared to be the Son of God in power according to the Spirit of holiness by his

resurrection from the dead, Jesus Christ
our Lord.

Paul says he has been called and "set apart for the gospel of
God." Your commonality with Paul and the centrality of your
calling is the gospel of God. This means that the gospel is to be
your all-consuming passion and focus. You are to be a gospel man
or a gospel woman.

The heart of the gospel is all about Jesus. Get to know Jesus.
The gospel of God is centered on God's Son, who existed with
the Father in equality for eternity—before the world even began.
Yet, there came a moment in history when the Son entered this
earth in the flesh at the incarnation. In His earthly existence,
He was historically "descended from David according to the
flesh." On earth, Jesus was thoroughly Jewish and a descendant
of David. It was expected from the Scriptures that the Messiah
would come from the line of David (2 Sam. 7:12–16; Is. 11:1–5),
and Jesus is the legitimate Messiah because in His earthly existence, He came from David's line.

Romans 1:4 describes His resurrection existence: "[Jesus]
was declared to be the Son of God in power according to the
Spirit of holiness by his resurrection from the dead, Jesus Christ
our Lord." Don't think this verse says that Jesus became the Son
of God at His resurrection. Obviously, He has always been the
Son of God. That's not what the verse means.

It's getting at a contrast between His earthly existence as the
incarnate Son of God and His heavenly existence as the incarnate
Son of God. His earthly existence in the flesh, as a descendant
of David, was one of humility and weakness eventually leading
to His death on the cross. In contrast, now He is the resurrected
"Son of God in power." Through His resurrection from the dead,
by the Holy Spirit, sin has been dealt with and Jesus is now the
reigning Lord. A more familiar passage getting at the same ex-
altation is Philippians 2:5–11, which speaks of Jesus taking on

human form and humbling Himself unto death on the cross. But after His resurrection, God exalted Him to the highest place of honor so that "every knee should bow ... and every tongue confess that Jesus Christ is Lord."

This is the gospel of God centered on Jesus Christ. May you be a gospel man or a gospel woman who is consumed with Jesus. He is your crucified, resurrected, and reigning Lord. May the Holy Spirit root you deep in the gospel, so that no matter the storms, Jesus will receive your passion, focus, obedience, and worship.

Memory Work

- Repeat 20 times 1 Corinthians 15:3–4 and mark the back of the card each time you say it.
- Don't forget to say the reference before and after you say the verse.
- Repeat Proverbs 4:23 once and mark the back of the card.

Day 7: The Gospel

When my oldest son was a freshman in high school, he interviewed me for an assignment concerning my hero and role model. We had a lot of fun because he knew who I would choose. Let me give you a summary of the questions asked and the quick answers.

1. Who is your role model? Jesus is my role model.
2. What characteristics does this person display? He is the great God-man who is perfect in all of His ways.
3. Why do you look up to this person? He loved me so much that He died for my sins and reconciled me to God.
4. What is your favorite quote from this person? John 14:6: "I am the way, and the truth, and the life. No one comes to the Father except through me."
5. What significant things has this person done in the world? Let's see, He created the world, defeated death, crushed Satan, and rose from the dead to never die again so that, through faith, people could live with God forever.
6. What kind of gift do you feel that this person gives to people? He gives us eternal life.
7. Is this person self-sacrificing in any way? Yes, He took on the sins of humanity and died on the cross bearing the wrath of God.
8. Has this person ever made any mistakes in the past? No, He lived a sinless, perfect life.

This is really not a fair pick for a role model. No matter who the other students chose as their role model, they will not compare to the greatness of Jesus. They might as well let my son go last, because if he goes first, it will make all the other heroes and role models seem a bit inferior. Jesus trumps all heroes and role models. Those who believe in Him have a deep conviction that He really is that much greater than all who have ever existed. Not only is it a deep-seated conviction, but true believers are not ashamed of the gospel of Jesus Christ.

Romans 1:16 says, "For I am not ashamed of the gospel, for it is the power of God for salvation to everyone who believes ..." The Christian makes the bold claim that Jesus is the Son of God who lived a sinless life and died to reconcile men to God through faith. He is now seated at the right hand of God, and everyone is called to repent and believe in Him as Savior and Lord of all. Most of the people you know in life probably don't cherish this gospel; they may even think it is crazy talk. You may feel that the gospel doesn't stack up to the elite and powerful vibe of the day. This may make you feel timid and, at times, ashamed of the gospel. But there is no need to be ashamed of the gospel because it contains the only power available to bring people to salvation through faith. There are no other options or ways to be reconciled to God; only through the power of the gospel of Jesus Christ can we be saved.

Once again, Romans 1:16 tells us: "For I am not ashamed of the gospel, for it is the power of God for salvation to everyone who believes ..." Contained within the gospel message is the omnipotence of God and His all-consuming power to save sinners. God's power in the gospel of Jesus' death and resurrection leads to people being saved from sin (Mt. 1:21), saved from God's wrath (Rom. 5:9), saved from their futile way of life (1 Pet. 1:18), saved from eternal separation from God (Eph. 2:12), and saved from death. Though the gospel may seem outlandish to some and absurd to others, you and I have seen God's power in the gospel to save and transform lives. Regardless of how the gospel may be perceived, you need not be ashamed, for it is the power of God for salvation.

Memory Work

- Repeat 15 times 1 Corinthians 15:3–4 and mark the back of the card each time you say it.
- Don't forget to say the reference before and after you say the verse.
- Repeat Proverbs 4:23 once and mark the back of the card.

Day 8: The Gospel

My best friend from junior high, high school, and college died in his early forties. We used to hang out all the time in Texas, and we both decided to go to the same college in Arkansas. We both became Christians in college, became pastors, and have the same name: Jason. One night he went to sleep and didn't wake up—he had a massive heart attack during the night. Once I heard the news, I booked a flight to Arkansas and flew back to our college town, where I hadn't been in about twenty years. It was very emotional, as I was at the Wesley Foundation where we both were discipled, where he had his dream job of leading the ministry. He was in his zone in ministry. He was married with two great daughters. And then he died. I saw him in the coffin with the Bible on his lap. I had a hard time processing this because you are not supposed to lose your best friends and your contemporaries until you are a bit older. I kept having flashbacks of him in the coffin, and two questions were hitting me—because I knew I would be there myself one day: (1) What is true? (2) What am I supposed to do?

Those are pretty good questions to ask yourself. What is true? What am I supposed to do? Start with the first question: What is true? You are saved through faith in Jesus Christ. Salvation is a gift from God to those who believe, not earned by deeds. This is not just faith in faith or a general faith in God, but faith in Jesus Christ, who has enabled sinners to have a right standing before God. It's not about working hard to get to God but freely receiving His grace as a gift by faith. Ephesians 2:8–9 says, "For by grace you have been saved through faith. And this is not your own doing; it is the gift of God, not a result of works, so that no one may boast."

Salvation is yours as a gift from God to be received, with no added works of our own. What is true? You are perfectly accepted by God through faith in the finished work of Jesus Christ. The pressure is off. You, a sinner, are declared to be perfectly righteous in God's sight through faith in Jesus Christ. You don't have to work hard to be accepted by God. Maybe you feel pressure from lots of people: parents, kids, teachers, or bosses. Most of them want you to perform to be accepted. But with God, the pressure is off, and the anxiety can be removed. You are accepted and declared perfect through faith in Christ.

> You are perfectly accepted by God through faith in the finished work of Jesus Christ. The pressure is off.

Now, on to the second pressing question, What am I supposed to do? The answer has already been stated and is quite simple: You are supposed to believe. Put your faith in Jesus Christ. Trying to earn your salvation will not get you right standing before God. Instead, respond to the work of God with a living faith in Jesus Christ.

- Put your faith in Jesus as your Savior. You are forgiven.
- Put your faith in Jesus through whom you are declared righteous. You are accepted.
- Put your faith in Jesus as your Redeemer. You are free from the bondage of sin and Satan.
- Put your faith in Jesus as your propitiation. God's favor is on you, not His wrath.
- Faith is not just a one-shot deal but an ongoing response to God's love for you in Jesus.

My childhood friend is now with Jesus. One day, I will be dead, as well, and you will be, too. There is no need for fear because God has revealed what is true and what you are supposed to do. Today is the day to walk in the truth of the gospel and believe in the Lord Jesus Christ.

Memory Work

- Repeat 10 times 1 Corinthians 15:3–4 and mark the back of the card each time you say it.
- Don't forget to say the reference before and after you say the verse.
- Repeat Proverbs 4:23 once and mark the back of the card.

The Holy Spirit

Ezekiel 36:27

"And I will put my Spirit within you, and cause you to walk in my statutes and be careful to obey my rules."

Day 9: The Holy Spirit

Oftentimes, we assume our lives would be so much better if Jesus were physically present on a daily basis to comfort and guide us. This desire will come true at the Second Coming, but it misses an important truth in the here and now. This lesson was taught to the first disciples on the last night Jesus was with them before His death. Jesus tells them He was about to go away, and they were fearful.

He encourages them with these words in John 16:7: "Nevertheless, I tell you the truth: it is to your advantage that I go away, for if I do not go away, the Helper will not come to you. But if I go, I will send him to you." Wow! Jesus seems to indicate that it was to the disciples' *advantage* (and ours) that He go away so that the Holy Spirit would come.

Perhaps Jesus just meant that, while He was on this earth, He could only be in one physical location at a time, but now the work of God could be all over the world through the Holy Spirit. That has to be a part of it, but I think another huge advantage was that the Holy Spirit would now live in them and carry on the work of Jesus through them. Jesus says in John 14:16–17, "And I will ask the Father, and he will give you another Helper, to be with you forever, even the Spirit of truth, whom the world cannot receive, because it neither sees him nor knows him. You know him, for he dwells with you and will be in you."

The third person of the Trinity, the Holy Spirit, now lives in believers. This is astounding and fulfills the promise of the Old Testament. In Ezekiel 36:26–27 God tells us, "And I will give you a new heart, and a new spirit I will put within you. And I will remove the heart of stone from your flesh and give you a heart of flesh. And I will put my Spirit within you, and cause you to walk in my statutes and be careful to obey my rules." You are living within a wonderful time in history; the Holy Spirit of God now lives within a believer forever.

The advantages of the indwelling of the Holy Spirit are manifold. For starters, the Holy Spirit came into your life and awakened you. He caused you to be born again and respond in repentance and faith to the gospel message. Now He empowers you to live a holy life and gives you gifts to serve the Church and the world. It may seem hard to love others, but you can do it because God has poured His love into your heart by the Holy Spirit, and you can, in turn, love others (Romans 5:5). In addition, you no longer have to keep giving in to sin, but by the Spirit's power, you can resist and put it to death (Romans 8:13).

The Holy Spirit brings you comfort and strength in the midst of suffering and pain (John 14:16). Even when the pain is too great to pray, the Holy Spirit will intercede for you according to the will of God (Romans 8:27). He enables you to know the truth of God and to recall the words of Jesus Christ (John 14:26). The Holy Spirit internally bears witness to remind you that you are an adopted and loved child of God (Romans 8:15–16). He empowers you to witness, and He brings conviction through the gospel of Jesus (John 16:8–11). As you can see, the Holy Spirit is constantly active for your good and God's glory.

Soon, you will be free from this corrupt world and at home with the Lord. As you wait, may you be strengthened and encouraged by the Holy Spirit today and until the day of Christ Jesus' return.

Memory Work

- Write out Ezekiel 36:27 along with the reference on the front of a 3x5 card.
- Write just the reference on the back of the card.
- Repeat it 25 times and mark the back of the card each time you say it.
- Say the reference before and after you say the verse.
- Return to Proverbs 4:23 and 1 Corinthians 15:3–4.
- Repeat each one time and mark the back of the card.

Day 10: The Holy Spirit

Galatians 5:16–17 and 24 have this to say:

> But I say, walk by the Spirit, and you will not gratify the desires of the flesh. For the desires of the flesh are against the Spirit, and the desires of the Spirit are against the flesh, for these are opposed to each other, to keep you from doing the things you want to do ... And those who belong to Christ Jesus have crucified the flesh with its passions and desires.

Your "flesh," which is your sinful desires and passions, has been crucified with Christ. This means that your old sinful way of living no longer has to dominate, because your "old self" has been killed at the cross. Romans 6:6 says, "We know that our old self was crucified with him in order that the body of sin might be brought to nothing, so that we would no longer be enslaved to sin." You are free in Christ Jesus. Yet, how can you account for your current struggle to live a godly life?

There is an internal war going on within believers between "the desires of the flesh" and "the desires of the Spirit." The flesh is the old me-centered, sinful way of doing life. The Spirit is the new, Christ-centered way of doing life. At your conversion, you were filled with the Holy Spirit and given a new heart, along with new overriding motivations and desires for a Christ-centered life. Yet, the old ways are waging war within, trying to exact control. James puts it this way in 4:1–2:

> What causes quarrels and what causes
> fights among you? Is it not this, that
> your passions are at war within you? You
> desire and do not have, so you murder.
> You covet and cannot obtain, so you fight
> and quarrel. You do not have, because
> you do not ask.

When you don't get what you want, your flesh tends to strike. However, it's not what you ultimately want, but sin warring within, as Paul says in Romans 7:22–23:

> For I delight in the law of God, in my inner
> being, but I see in my members another
> law waging war against the law of my
> mind and making me captive to the law of
> sin that dwells in my members.

As a believer, you truly want what the Holy Spirit wants, but your old ways are trying to make a comeback.

The good news is that you can be led by the Spirit, which means that you really can obey. You can tell your old sinful ways, "You are dead. You have no power over me." No matter how tempting your old ways seem, you don't have to give in because you are led by the Spirit. You have the power of the Holy Spirit to turn away from sin and obey the Word of God. As you go out into the world today, your charge is to "walk by the Spirit."

Practically speaking, this means that you live a life of full strength and full dependence. By the power of the Holy Spirit,

> As you go out into the world today, your charge is to "walk by the Spirit."

you exert your will and effort to turn away from sin and turn to a life of righteousness. Holiness is an act of full strength, but it's also a life of complete and utter dependence. This dependence is expressed in calling out to God on a daily basis through prayer to strengthen you to walk by the Spirit. It's a dependence upon God's Word and God's people to spur you on in a Spirit-led life for the glory of God. Today is your day to once again "walk by the Spirit" in full strength and full dependence.

Memory Work

- Repeat 20 times Ezekiel 36:27 and mark the back of the card each time you say it.
- Don't forget to say the reference before and after you say the verse.
- Repeat Proverbs 4:23 and 1 Corinthians 15:3–4 once and mark the back of the cards.

Day 11: The Holy Spirit

May the Holy Spirit impress upon you today, through the Word of God, that you are an adopted child of God. Romans 8:14 tells us, "For all who are led by the Spirit of God are sons of God." This is not a mystical leading of the Holy Spirit in making big decisions about what job to take or whom to marry. The context shows that this leading of the Holy Spirit is a leading into a life of holiness. Romans 8:13 bears this out: "For if you live according to the flesh you will die, but if by the Spirit you put to death the deeds of the body, you will live." The Spirit enables you to kill sin and leads you into a life of obedience and holiness. Those who are led in this way are called "sons of God." You are a child of God who is led by the Spirit of God.

Romans 8:15 says, "For you did not receive the spirit of slavery to fall back into fear, but you have received the Spirit of adoption as sons, by whom we cry, 'Abba! Father!'" You don't have to fear the wrath and condemnation of God to an eternity in hell because you can't keep the law. Christ kept the law in your place, died for your sins, and was raised to give you a new life reconciled to God. You embraced this gospel by faith as the Holy Spirit awakened you. At conversion you received the Holy Spirit, who affirms that you are no longer a slave to sin but an adopted child of God.

Only Jesus is the natural Son of God and He has been for eternity. But those who are united with Christ have now "received the Spirit of adoption as sons." The Spirit produces a cry or a prayer in you by which you say, "Abba! Father." Abba is an Aramaic word for "father." Just as Jesus called God His Father, so you can now interact with God in the same intimate way. You have that intimacy created by the Spirit where you can call God, "Abba, Father." You are a dependent child of God who can call out to Him, the One who loves you so much that He adopted you as His own.

This intimate, close connection is often depicted in an earthly adoption. It is natural for an adopted child to take on the new family's last name. It's why I can say to my adopted daughter, Mary, "You are a Lancaster now." There is such a close connection between her and our family that she is now one of us. But there is a special legal connection she

> You are a dependent child of God who can call out to Him, the One who loves you so much that He adopted you as His own.

has with me as her father. Through all the legal proceedings, she had to not only take on our last name, but also my first name as her middle name. All of her documents showed that her official name was now "Mary Jason Lancaster." Isn't that cool? Now, we don't want her to grow up with a boy's middle name, so we changed it. But I know of the special connection between her and me. In a similar way, you are in the family of God with all of your brothers and sisters in Christ, but there is this special connection you have with the Father, who loves you and calls you His own. And your response is to cry, "Abba, Father."

You can actually experience this connection to the Father by the Holy Spirit. Romans 8:16 states, "The Spirit himself bears witness with our spirit that we are children of God." If you are a believer, the Holy Spirit ministers to your spirit that you are a child of God. It is not a ministry of fear but one of confirmation and assurance that you are God's adopted child. May the ministry of the Holy Spirit assure you today that you are an adopted child of God, and may you cry out, "Abba, Father."

Memory Work

- Repeat 15 times Ezekiel 36:27 and mark the back of the card each time you say it.
- Don't forget to say the reference before and after you say the verse.
- Repeat Proverbs 4:23 and 1 Corinthians 15:3–4 once and mark the back of the cards.

Day 12: The Holy Spirit

Who owns you? If you are a believer, the Bible indicates that God owns you. "You are not your own, for you were bought with a price. So glorify God in your body" (1 Corinthians 6:19–20). Yet, practically speaking, sometimes you act as though you own you.

You spend money like it's yours to spend. You waste time like it's yours to waste. You make career, school, and relationship decisions as if they are yours alone to make. You do things with your mind and body like they are yours to use however you wish. And when life doesn't go the way you want it to, you complain, as if your life was even yours in the first place.

The truth is that you don't own you: God owns you, and that is good news. This truth can free you from the bondage of your own control, expectations, and manipulation of life. This truth will free you from your greatest enemy—you. Since God owns you, the pressure's off! The pressure is off of you trying to control life the way you want or to set expectations that must be met or to manipulate life for your own desired outcome. You are His, and He is in control. He can do with you whatever He wants. Your only response is to trust Him, to release control, and to simply live for the One who owns you.

> The truth is that you don't own you: God owns you, and that is good news.

Ephesians 1:13 tells us: "In him you also, when you heard the word of truth, the gospel of your salvation, and believed in him, were sealed with the promised Holy Spirit." What does it mean that you were "sealed with the Holy Spirit"? A seal is a brand or a mark of ownership. You were marked or sealed on the inside with the Holy Spirit. Second Corinthians 1:21–22 states, "And it is God who establishes us with you in Christ, and has anointed us, and who has also put his seal on us and given us his Spirit in our hearts as a guarantee." The Holy Spirit, the third person of the Trinity, has been placed in your heart as a seal of ownership. If you are a believer, you don't need to be sealed with the Holy Spirit again; it is a done deal. At your conversion, you were permanently sealed with the Holy Spirit as God's possession. If He has sealed you, you will make it from here (earth) to there (heaven) because you are His own property. The lyrics of the hymn "Come, Thou Fount" declare:

> Prone to wander, Lord, I feel it,
> Prone to leave the God I love;
> Here's my heart, O take and seal it,
> Seal it for Thy courts above.

You are prone to wander and prone to leave the God you love. However, God has sealed your heart with the Holy Spirit to keep you on track, so that you will reach God's courts above.

You don't own you: God owns you, and that is good news. Since God owns you, the pressure's off! There is no more pressure to control your life the way you want or to set strict expectations or manipulate life for your own desired outcome. God is your owner, so live to praise Him in your heart, words, and actions today, for His glory.

Memory Work

- Repeat 10 times Ezekiel 36:27 and mark the back of the card each time you say it.
- Don't forget to say the reference before and after you say the verse.
- Repeat Proverbs 4:23 and 1 Corinthians 15:3–4 once and mark the back of the cards.

The Word

2 Timothy 3:16

All Scripture is breathed out by God and profitable for teaching, for re-proof, for correction, and for training in righteousness.

Day 13: The Word

After college, I decided to go to seminary, but I did not know where I should go. I visited schools in Atlanta, Durham, Chicago, Los Angeles, and Dallas. I spent a lot of time in prayer, basically saying, "God, if You will just tell me what to do, then I will do it." I eventually chose to attend seminary in Dallas. At the end of my seminary career, I was locked in on someone I wanted to marry, but I was freaking out because my parents had been divorced, and I didn't know how to date. I spent a lot of time praying, "God, if You will just tell me what to do, then I will do it." I eventually married the girl who is now my wife.

Maybe you are trying to make some big decisions in your life, and you are hoping to figure out what God wants you to do. You may be praying, "God, if You will just tell me what to do, then I will do it." It can be about small things or big things, but if God would just somehow reveal to you what He wants you to do, then you would do it. Let me just stop: Would you *really* do what God tells you to do with your life? I'm a little skeptical.

Let's say there is a guy who really wants to ask a girl out, and he is praying and asking God whether or not he should do it. He thinks, "God, if You will just tell me what to do, then I will do it." What if God said, "I've already told you so many things in My Word, and I want you to grow in Me, but you are not listening. And now you want Me to speak to you about going out with, loving, and leading some girl—when you can't even lead yourself?"

Sometimes you want God to speak to you and to guide you, but you aren't too eager to pay attention to what He has already said. You fail to see what His Word is telling you on a regular basis—spoken by the Holy Spirit and infused with wisdom from others. You don't want to hear His truth, and you act as if He is not speaking at all.

> As you respond to God's Word, you will notice that God is shaping and leading you by His Word and His Spirit.

Yet, God speaks through His Word all the time if you are willing to listen. Second Timothy 3:16 says, "All Scripture is breathed out by God and profitable for teaching, for reproof, for correction, and for training in righteousness." All of God's Word is profitable for your life. From Genesis to Revelation, God is speaking truth to you so that you might know Him and walk in His ways. Sometimes His Word rebukes and corrects. Other times it encourages and comforts. All in all, God is using His Word to train you to live a life of godliness by walking in His ways. God is speaking to you all the time through His Word. Are you listening?

As you respond to God's Word, you will notice that God is shaping and leading you by His Word and His Spirit. That's what you want when it's all said and done. When you pray, "God, just tell me what You want me to do and I will do it," that prayer is answered as you are shaped

> . . . come to the Lord *on a daily basis*, before His Word, with a heart that has a listening disposition.

by the revealed will of God in His Word. And over time, God's Word will shape your big decisions in life. All the details of your college major and your marriage and your career will come at the right time through community, prayer, wisdom, and discernment. You need to come to the Lord *on a daily basis*, before His

Word, with a heart that has a listening disposition. God wants to speak to you today. Will you listen?

Memory Work

- Write out 2 Timothy 3:16 along with the reference on the front of a 3x5 card.
- Write just the reference on the back of the card.
- Repeat it 25 times and mark the back of the card each time you say it.
- Say the reference before and after you say the verse.
- Return to Proverbs 4:23, 1 Corinthians 15:3–4, and Ezekiel 36:27.
- Repeat each one time and mark the back of the card.

Day 14: The Word

Let me tell you the best news ever for improving your quality of life. God has set a plan in place to redeem you from His wrath and deliver you from sin through Jesus Christ. He communicated His plan to you in His Word. If you repent of your sins and put your faith in Jesus Christ, you will be saved. Along with this gospel, He has communicated everything you need for life and godliness.

The Bible tells about how God is in control and sovereign, how He is working for your good, and how you can live to be happy in God. Yet you probably don't always read it as you should. You may go to website after website and research ways to lose weight, be happier, raise your kids right, get a date, make money, and be successful. But you have God speaking truth to you every day through His Word, and yet you don't read it as you should.

Rather than heaping up guilt and shame for your lack of time spent in God's Word, focus on the happiness and joy you can get by immersing yourself in the Bible. Psalm 119 is filled with such joy as it demonstrates the psalmist's passionate pursuit of God and His Word. Psalm 119:1 says:

> Blessed are those whose way is blameless,
> who walk in the law of the Lord!

The psalmist points out people who are walking in the favor of God. There is a certain amount of blessedness, happiness, and joy that can only be found in walking in the "law of the Lord."

The Israelites were to view the Old Testament Law, such as the Ten Commandments, as instructions to increase their happiness, not as restrictions to decrease their happiness. When God's children strive for a life of integrity and blamelessness in line with God's Word, the blessing of God's favor rests upon them. Perhaps you have experienced this blessedness in your own life. Maybe after a long struggle with sin, you finally repented and decided to obey God. At first, it might have been painful to resist temptation, but you knew that you were walking in a way that pleased the Lord and that gave you joy. Psalm 119:2 says:

> Blessed are those who keep his testimonies,
> who seek him with their whole heart.

The psalmist continues to emphasize the blessedness of those who "keep his testimonies" and seek the Lord "with their whole heart." These are the people who are not just seeking a book full of laws or instructions on how to conduct their lives but who are seeking God with "their whole heart." They understand that true happiness and blessedness lie in God and His Word.

> When God's children strive for a life of integrity and blamelessness in line with God's Word, the blessing of God's favor rests upon them.

Sometimes, you may have a hard time believing that God can make you completely happy in Himself. Perhaps you think that happiness is found in God plus other things. So, you'll take God, but you will also seek after comfort, security, and happiness outside of God. However, true joy is found in seeking God with your whole heart. It comes through surrendering your whole will and life to Him. You can cultivate seeking God with your whole heart, immersing yourself in the Word of God. Even on the days you are not convinced God and His Word can completely satisfy, sit down by faith, open the

Bible, and dive in. May God surprise you once again through His life-giving and joy-filling Word.

Memory Work

- Repeat 20 times 2 Timothy 3:16 and mark the back of the card each time you say it.
- Don't forget to say the reference before and after you say the verse.
- Return to Proverbs 4:23, 1 Corinthians 15:3–4, and Ezekiel 36:27.
- Repeat each one time and mark the back of each card.

Day 15: The Word

What would it look like to come to God's Word on a daily basis and have a listening disposition? What if you approached God with an eagerness to hear and respond to His Word? I don't know about you, but I can come to God's Word and be so far off. My mind is distracted with many cares. Rather than fostering heart engagement, I can fall into a boring routine of robotic reading. What can help?

Let me suggest a simple prayer that I learned many years ago from Pastor John Piper. The acronym is I.O.U.S.[1]

I – "Incline my heart to your testimonies and not to selfish gain." (Psalm 119:36)
Start by asking God to turn your heart toward His Word and away from selfish pursuits.

O – "Open my eyes that I may behold wonderful things out of your law." (Psalm 119:18)
Often God's Word seems unimpressive, so you are asking to see His Word as indeed wonderful.

1. John Piper interview, "Ask Pastor John," 2/7/2017, Episode 999. "How Do I Pray the Bible?" Audio transcript. https://www.desiringgod.org /interviews/how-do-i-pray-the-bible. By John Piper. © Desiring God Foundation. Source: desiringGod.org.

U – "Unite my heart to fear your name."
(Psalm 86:11)
A healthy fear of God puts you in a
position to hear from your authoritative
heavenly Father.

S – "Satisfy [me] in the morning with
your steadfast love that [I] may rejoice
and be glad all my days."
(Psalm 90:14)
Ultimately, you want to take joy in God
and His love for you. We are all dull and
in need of God's grace to hear His Word
and respond.

Take some extra time today before your Scripture memory work to pray through each letter of the I.O.U.S. Prayerfully set yourself up to hear and respond to God's Word.

Memory Work

- Repeat 15 times 2 Timothy 3:16 and mark the back of the card each time you say it.
- Don't forget to say the reference before and after you say the verse.
- Return to Proverbs 4:23, 1 Corinthians 15:3–4, and Ezekiel 36:27.
- Repeat each one time and mark the back of each card.

Day 16: The Word

You must be careful to avoid starting to think that reading the Word of God is enough, that you don't need to make a response of obedience. James 1:22 tells us: "But be doers of the word, and not hearers only, deceiving yourselves." You can be deceived into thinking that just hearing a sermon or reading the Bible equals obedience. Spirit-empowered obedience is the appropriate response to the Word of God.

Jesus demonstrates the importance of obedience to His words in a stunning parable, found in Matthew 7:24–27:

> Everyone then who hears these words of mine and does them will be like a wise man who built his house on the rock. And the rain fell, and the floods came, and the winds blew and beat on that house, but it did not fall, because it had been founded on the rock. And everyone who hears these words of mine and does not do them will be like a foolish man who built his house on the sand. And the rain fell, and the floods came, and the winds blew and beat against that house, and it fell, and great was the fall of it.

The focus here is on the builders and what they built. The builder who built his house on the solid foundation of rock is pointing to the one who heard Jesus' words and actually obeyed them. The storm of God's future judgment came, and they stood firm because they had a converted heart that produced obedience.

But the builder who built his house on the sand is the foolish one who hears Jesus' words but does not do them. The judgment of God came, and the disobedient life they were building fell with a great crash. Both groups heard, but hearing was not enough. If you do His words, they lead to life, but throwing off His words leads to destruction in hell.

> If you are hearing the Word and not obeying, you are building your life apart from Jesus.

Why would you want to ignore obedience to God's Word and build your life apart from Him? Of course, it's easier and more popular to just strike out on your own. But you have to see that, no matter how well things are going right now, there will come a day of destruction, of eternal punishment in hell.

Once, I had some construction done in my house when my kitchen floor was replaced. In clearing the way for the new floor, they had to rip out the current floor, which then progressed into ripping out four floors. The first layer was a retro floor, from when the house was built in the 1950s. It was probably not replaced until the late '60s or early '70s with a groovy floor that looked like a sparkly disco ball. The third layer was an awesome, bright, yellow-patterned floor. Then, probably in the '90s, they went with a floor that was plain and bland. Regardless of how perfect each new layer appeared at the time of installation, in time our builder ripped up all the layers and replaced them with our nice, new floor. However, no matter how cool *we* think *our* new floor is, one day it will also be destroyed.

If you are hearing the Word and not obeying, you are building your life apart from Jesus. You may be doing that now, and your life may look as good as my new kitchen floor. Things are going well for you, and you are generally happy with what you are building. But a day of destruction is coming for all those who refuse to hear Jesus' words and obey what He says. A day of judgment is coming for all those who refuse to obey out of a converted heart. May you be one who is eager to hear the Word and obey by the power of the Spirit.

Memory Work

- Repeat 10 times 2 Timothy 3:16 and mark the back of the card each time you say it.
- Don't forget to say the reference before and after you say the verse.
- Return to Proverbs 4:23, 1 Corinthians 15:3–4, and Ezekiel 36:27.
- Repeat each one time and mark the back of each card.

Love

1 John 4:7

Beloved, let us love one another, for love is from God, and whoever loves has been born of God and knows God.

Day 17: Love

It's hard to love. Perhaps you can love in bursts and spurts, but to love over the long haul is very difficult. I could give you some tips and tricks, but they would probably fall flat when you felt unable or apathetic. Methods on how to love can be helpful, but you have a greater need than methodology; you have a need for theology. That's why you must go deeper into theology and deeper into the origin of love, seen in the very character of God Himself.

The apostle John says in 1 John 4:7, "Beloved, let us love one another, for love is from God, and whoever loves has been born of God and knows God." The origin and source of love are God. Not only is love *from* God, but also God *is* love. First John 4:16 says, "So we have come to know and to believe the love that God has for us. God is love, and whoever abides in love abides in God, and God abides in him." The key attribute of God is love, and He has expressed His love to us through Jesus Christ.

First John 4:9–10, 14 states:

> In this the love of God was made manifest among us, that God sent his only Son into the world, so that we might live through him. In this is love, not that we have loved God but that he loved us and sent his Son to be the propitiation for our sins ... And we have seen and testify that the Father has sent his Son to be the Savior of the world.

How do you know that God loves you? Because He sent His Son, Jesus Christ, to die on the cross for your sins. Jesus took on flesh in the incarnation because God wanted to express His love to you. More specifically, His love for you was shown by the sacrifice of Jesus as a propitiation for sinners. *Propitiation* simply means a sacrifice to turn away anger or wrath. God's anger was against you for your sins, and if not dealt with, it would have led to eternal separation from Him. But God's love was expressed in pouring out His wrath fully on His Son on the cross instead of on you. Now if you look to Jesus in faith, you will find forgiveness. There is no greater news in the world to embrace than the fact you are completely loved and forgiven through faith in Jesus Christ.

Part of John's argument is that the substitutionary death of Jesus should lead believers to love one another as He has loved us. First John 4:11–12 encourages us, "Beloved, if God so loved us, we also ought to love one another. No one has ever seen God; if we love one another, God abides in us and his love is perfected in us." You can now love others because you have been loved through the cross of Christ. The sacrificial love that has been expressed to you, you can now spill out in sacrificial ways toward others. God does not reject you but loves and accepts you in Jesus, and now you can do the same with others.

Are you starting to see why theology matters? You can have all the conflict-resolution skills in the world, but when someone rejects you, what happens? You are still left with the personal knowledge that you are completely accepted by the One who dearly and deeply loves you. God is the One who has the reason to reject you, but because of Jesus' propitiation on the cross, He accepts you and loves you. Now you can love others out of this position of acceptance and grace. God is love, and His love has been expressed to you. Now, by God's power, His love can be expressed through you. The ultimate motivator to love is God's love.

Memory Work

- Write out 1 John 4:7 along with the reference on the front of a 3x5 card.
- Write just the reference on the back of the card.
- Repeat it 25 times and mark the back of the card each time you say it.
- Say the reference before and after you say the verse.
- Return to Proverbs 4:23, 1 Corinthians 15:3–4, Ezekiel 36:27, and 2 Timothy 3:16.
- Repeat each one time and mark the back of each card.

Day 18: Love

You probably want to accomplish great things in your life—and that is not a bad thing. You want to see the fulfillment of your dreams and visions. This can cause you to work hard and to go all-out in their pursuit. But if along the way you fail to engage others with love, it all comes to nothing. We can do great things, even great things for God, but if we don't have love then it's all cancelled out. It means nothing. Greatness – Love = Nothing.

That's the way the apostle Paul begins the famous love chapter of 1 Corinthians 13. Paul wrote to a church in Corinth that had great spiritual gifts but were lacking in love. They were bursting with spiritual gifts, especially the more expressive gifts such as speaking in tongues, prophesying, and faith. Yet, while exercising their gifts, they failed to adequately love. Their use of the gifts was more about showing off than building up others. Paul doesn't throw out the gifts, but he shows that they are worthless without the greater emphasis on love. Once again, Greatness – Love = Nothing.

In the first three verses, notice the great abilities and accomplishments that can be done for God. First Corinthians 13:1–3 states, "If I speak in the tongues of men and of angels, but have not love, I am a noisy gong or a clanging cymbal." A person can speak in tongues, but without love, it's just noise. "And if I have prophetic powers, and understand all mysteries and all knowledge, and if I have all faith, so as to remove mountains, but have not love, I am nothing." Even the gift of prophecy or the great gift of faith that can move mountains is nothing without love. "If I give away all I have, and if I deliver up my body to be burned, but have not love, I gain nothing." Giving away all your possessions to serve the Lord and even sacrificing your body to death in martyrdom gains nothing if you don't have love. Greatness – Love = Nothing.

There is this drive within most of us to accomplish great things in life and great things for God. But if we leave out love, it comes to nothing. First Corinthians 13 always tends to slow me down and give me a picture of who I want to become. In my natural, unrestrained state, I am driven to accomplish great things for God. Thus, slowing down to love is difficult, but it also brings perspective. The silly image I have to demonstrate this concept is a famous NBA basketball player. He played the game of his life in a pivotal game seven to help his team win the championship. A few hours later, his picture was taken eating breakfast with friends and family at Denny's. He wasn't out clubbing and partying with all the celebrities, but rather having a simple meal. It's a contrasting image of glory on the podium to love around the table at Denny's.

It's the winner's podium, the confetti, the parties, and the highlight reels that many people tend to focus on. You get pumped about utilizing your gifts to maximum potential. You get excited about exercising your faith, giving sacrificially and even laying your life on the line for Jesus. But sitting around and loving other people is so boring, bland, and mundane. Yet, living a life of love is what it's all about. A mother plans a great Disney vacation, but when it's over, she still has the everyday task to love. A student goes on a summer mission trip, but she must still come home and love her parents. An author launches a great book about love, but he still has to love on a daily basis. Greatness – Love = Nothing. However, when we inject love in our lives, it brings glory to God, because love is what it is all about.

Memory Work

- Repeat 20 times 1 John 4:7 and mark the back of the card each time you say it.
- Don't forget to say the reference before and after you say the verse.
- Return to Proverbs 4:23, 1 Corinthians 15:3–4, Ezekiel 36:27, and 2 Timothy 3:16.
- Repeat each one time and mark the back of each card.

Day 19: Love

First Corinthians 13:4–7 says:

> Love is patient and kind; love does not
> envy or boast; it is not arrogant or rude.
> It does not insist on its own way; it is not
> irritable or resentful; it does not rejoice at
> wrongdoing, but rejoices with the truth.
> Love bears all things, believes all things,
> hopes all things, endures all things.

This description of love could be a beautiful description of the love of God. For example, let's start out by inserting *Jesus* in the place of *love*. "*Jesus* is patient and kind; *Jesus* does not envy or boast; *Jesus* is not arrogant or rude." *Jesus* loved the Father and others perfectly. Yet, this is not a description of God's love; it is supposed to be a description of your own love. Instead of inserting Jesus' name, now insert your own. I'll use mine for example: "*Jason* is patient and kind; *Jason* does not envy or boast; *Jason* is not arrogant or rude." I'm getting uncomfortable and convicted because I know I fall short of the standards of love.

How are we supposed to pull this off? You can't, but God can. Two thoughts here:

1. Since Jesus does not fall short of love's standards, He keeps them for you before a holy God. Through faith, you can be accepted by God because Jesus loved perfectly in life and in death. Through His life, death, and resurrection you can be counted loving in Christ, before God.

2. Now, as a believer, the Holy Spirit gives you the ability to imitate His love. You have been given a new heart because the Holy Spirit has been poured into your heart. Romans 5:5 states, "... God's love has been poured into our hearts through the Holy Spirit who has been given to us." The Christian should never say, "I can't love." You *can* love because God's love has been poured into your life and now overflows to others.

You are called to love others from your heart. Notice that most of the descriptions of love include both actions and attitudes, which really gets at the heart. Look again at verses 4–7:

> Love is patient and kind; love does not envy or boast; it is not arrogant or rude. It does not insist on its own way; it is not irritable or resentful; it does not rejoice at wrongdoing, but rejoices with the truth. Love bears all things, believes all things, hopes all things, endures all things.

Love is a selfless sacrifice. If you base your love on what you can get out of it or how it makes you feel, you will have a hard time loving.

> Through faith, you can be accepted by God because Jesus loved perfectly in life and in death.

It's hard to be patient when someone won't get their act together, but God has been patient with you. Maybe you don't feel like being kind to others because they don't deserve it, but God has been kind to you even though you don't deserve it. Arrogance and rudeness go hand in hand, but humility and courtesy come through denying yourself.

Notice in the middle that love does not insist on its own way; it's not about you or your rights but about serving others. Love is not irritable in the sense that it is easily set off, but instead, it lets stuff slide. Love is not resentful in the sense that it doesn't keep a record of wrongs to be brought up at just the right time.

When someone reaps what they have sown, it's easy to rejoice at wrongdoing. But not love. It takes another path and only rejoices with the truth; it "bears all things, believes all things, hopes all things, endures all things."

Memory Work

- Repeat 15 times 1 John 4:7 and mark the back of the card each time you say it.
- Don't forget to say the reference before and after you say the verse.
- Return to Proverbs 4:23, 1 Corinthians 15:3–4, Ezekiel 36:27, and 2 Timothy 3:16.
- Repeat each one time and mark the back of each card.

Day 20: Love

Love is often sacrificial in nature. Consider the startling and radical words of Jesus in Matthew 5:43–44: "You have heard that it was said, 'You shall love your neighbor and hate your enemy.' But I say to you, Love your enemies and pray for those who persecute you." The Old Testament said to "love your neighbor," and many of the teachers of Jesus' day had an extended version that said, "... and hate your enemies." Jesus counters the popular teaching of the day with a call to love and pray for your enemies.

Jesus follows with some motivation in Matthew 5:45: "So that you may be sons of your Father who is in heaven. For he makes his sun rise on the evil and on the good, and sends rain on the just and on the unjust." You can't love your enemies because you are a good person, but because you have been changed from the inside out and you now reflect the character of your Father in heaven. God consistently loves those who are wicked and evil to Him and to others. By His grace, He causes the sun to rise and the rain to pour even for the benefit of his enemies. Why would He do that? Because they are people created in His image, people who are valuable to Him and whom He desires to be saved. If that is how God consistently treats the wicked, we are to imitate our Father in heaven and do the same.

Jesus continues in Matthew 5:46–47: "For if you love those who love you, what reward do you have? Do not even the tax collectors do the same? And if you greet only your brothers, what more are you doing than others? Do not even the Gentiles do the same?" Jesus is calling His followers to go above and beyond the way the world functions. Even the despised tax collectors can love those who love them back. And even the pagan Gentiles know how to greet those with whom they are connected. There is no special heavenly favor for doing what comes naturally. When we love those who love us back or hang out with those with whom we get along, what more are we doing than others? We are supposed to be a distinct people who are set apart and function in the radical norms of the kingdom.

Jesus pushes us to perfection in Matthew 5:48: "You therefore must be perfect, as your heavenly Father is perfect." I see this no differently than the calls in the Bible to be holy as God is holy (Lev. 20:26; 1 Pet. 1:16). Once you see that you can't keep God's holy standard, you cry out to Him over your sin and find forgiveness in the cross of Christ. This brings you to the perfection of Christ and His righteousness in which you are clothed, so in the eyes of God you are perfect in Him. Now you are to live out this reality in a life of holiness, pursuing your Father's perfection by His grace and power. Part of this is reflecting the heart and character of God to love and pray for your enemies.

Take some time to think about anyone who may be opposed to you or even those who are just difficult to get along with. Take some time to pray for them, and ask God for wisdom on specific ways you can love them today.

Memory Work

- Repeat 10 times 1 John 4:7 and mark the back of the card each time you say it.
- Don't forget to say the reference before and after you say the verse.
- Return to Proverbs 4:23, 1 Corinthians 15:3–4, Ezekiel 36:27, and 2 Timothy 3:16.
- Repeat each one time and mark the back of each card.

Witness

Acts 1:8

"But you will receive power
when the Holy Spirit has come upon
you, and you will be my witnesses in
Jerusalem and in all Judea and
Samaria, and to the end of the
earth."

Day 21: Witness

The gospel is not meant to terminate on the believer, but it is to be shared. After the death and resurrection of Jesus, the Church was active and bold in sharing the gospel. The book of Acts depicts the acts of Jesus from heaven by the Holy Spirit through His people to build His Church. This building of the Church through proclamation finds its root in the commission of Jesus before He left this earth. In Acts 1:8, Jesus said, "But you will receive power when the Holy Spirit has come upon you, and you will be my witnesses in Jerusalem and in all Judea and Samaria, and to the end of the earth." The implications of this important verse explained the power of God behind the mission that is still available to believers today.

In verse 8, He says, "But you will receive power when the Holy Spirit has come upon you . . ." The mission was going to be one enabled by grace. The Holy Spirit of God was going to empower them with a mighty strength and boldness to carry out the work. Following Christ is a work of grace from start to finish. You are saved by God's grace through repentance and faith in the work of Jesus on your behalf that you do not deserve. And you persevere and do His work by grace. His grace transforms you into a dwelling of the Holy Spirit, and you are now a person empowered by the Holy Spirit to proclaim the gospel. The mission is not one empowered by your own self-will, but it is empowered by God's Holy Spirit. God not only wants you to tell others about the great work of God through Jesus, but He also gives you the power to do it.

Verse 8 continues: " . . . and you will be my witnesses in Jerusalem and in all Judea and Samaria, and to the end of the earth." The enabling power of the Holy Spirit was to be a witness of Jesus. The idea of "witness" is to give an eyewitness account of what has been seen and heard. The apostles could do this with their firsthand experience of the death and resurrection of Jesus Christ. You do it based upon the historical facts of the death and resurrection of Jesus and the Holy Spirit's awakening and empowering. You are to witness to the fact of the historical life, death, and resurrection of Jesus Christ. You should tell others what happened, but you must also give them the biblical interpretation of the facts—that Jesus died in place of sinners, that He bears the wrath of God for sinners, and that He offers His perfect righteousness to sinners. Don't stop there, but go on to speak of the good news that people separated from God can be reconciled to Him through repentance and faith in Jesus. Talk about the historical reality of the cross and the modern-day interpretation for every human being.

And don't even stop there. You are a witness to the fact of something that has happened in you. You have repented of your sins and you have found forgiveness in Jesus Christ. Tell your personal story of being saved from your sins and the life you have in Christ. Tell your story in such a way that it still focuses on the acts of Jesus. But don't forget when you speak with someone about Jesus, it's not up to your strength and wisdom, but God's. His power should give you the boldness to step out and proclaim the good news of Jesus Christ—even today.

Memory Work

- Write out Acts 1:8 along with the reference on the front of a 3x5 card.
- Write just the reference on the back of the card.
- Repeat it 25 times and mark the back of the card each time you say it.
- Say the reference before and after you say the verse.
- Return to Proverbs 4:23, 1 Corinthians 15:3–4, Ezekiel 36:27, 2 Timothy 3:16, and 1 John 4:7.
- Repeat each one time and mark the back of each card.

Day 22: Witness

Return once again to Acts 1:8: "But you will receive power when the Holy Spirit has come upon you, and you will be my witnesses in Jerusalem and in all Judea and Samaria, and to the end of the earth."

The disciples were empowered by the Holy Spirit to be witnesses starting in Jerusalem, then to spread out to Judea and Samaria, then to the ends of the earth. These locations are basically the structure of the book of Acts. The first seven chapters have the gospel going throughout Jerusalem. Then, chapters 8 through 12 have the gospel in Judea and Samaria, and the rest of the book takes the gospel to Rome. Then, the book abruptly ends, but the work is not finished, as the witnesses are to speak the gospel throughout the world.

Notice that the gospel is not just a Jewish gospel, but it was to go throughout the world and invite all into the kingdom through repentance and faith in Jesus. God's love is for people in Jerusalem, Judea, Samaria, and the nations. The gospel is not just to be proclaimed to a few, select people, but to the whole world. Think about this broad gospel exposure in terms of the way a family cares for one another.

A few years ago, a couple of my kids were sick around the same time. First, the illness struck my four-year-old daughter. We offered her care and comfort. Then, as soon as she was better, my eight-year-old daughter got sick, and we offered her care and comfort. We were ready to do the same for the rest of our kids if they got sick, as well. But what if we had only limited our care to the first kid or got tired after caring for the two of them? What if our compassion had limits and only stretched so far? That would be absurd, because we care about them all. God cares about the people of the nations, and He didn't want the apostles to narrow their focus to just the Jews, nor does He want us to narrow our focus to people like us while we ignore the rest.

It's sometimes difficult to see the necessity of broad gospel exposure, especially for those who live in big cities. As cities are made up of people with diverse religions and backgrounds, it's tempting to think that the gospel is only for us Christians. Maybe you are hesitant to share with your Muslim or Hindu friends, colleagues, and fellow students. You are hesitant to share with the peaceful Zen person, the happy Bahai person, the confident secularist, or the cultural Christian. If you are not sharing the gospel with them, with whom does Jesus have in mind that we share it? The gospel is for them! You have been called to love people from all cultures and religious backgrounds by sharing the gospel with boldness.

Start off your day with this simple prayer: "Lord, I am at Your disposal today. Please show me whom I should talk to about Jesus." You will be shocked by how your witnessing desire and power come alive.

You may have taken your child on a play date to the park with the same moms for months. But this time is different. In dependence upon the Holy Spirit, you feel inwardly compelled to tell the Hindu woman about Jesus Christ. Or you may have talked to the same people over lunch at school or work for weeks, but now you feel compelled to speak the gospel. I love and hate this feeling all at the same time. I love that the Lord is leading and prompting me to speak about Jesus, but I hate it because, in my flesh, I resist it so much. But what an exciting life to lead—one empowered and led by the Holy Spirit to carry out kingdom work. Live your days with an open mind and heart to the leading and the empowering of the Holy Spirit to proclaim the gospel to the nations.

Memory Work

- Repeat 20 times Acts 1:8 and mark the back of the card each time you say it.
- Don't forget to say the reference before and after you say the verse.
- Return to Proverbs 4:23, 1 Corinthians 15:3–4, Ezekiel 36:27, 2 Timothy 3:16, and 1 John 4:7.
- Repeat each one time and mark the back of each card.

Day 23: Witness

At my former church, the members have a certain ethos that describes who they are and who they want to become as followers of Jesus Christ. Part of the ethos is that they want to cultivate a culture of people living out a "pervasive gospel." A culture full of people who are all about growing in the gospel and who want to see others impacted by the gospel locally and globally. This culture of a pervasive gospel is what the apostle Paul was cultivating in the church in Rome. His letter focused on the good news of Jesus and how the church could grow and see the gospel spread. Paul says in Romans 15:20, "I make it my ambition to preach the gospel." The specifics of his ambition had him preaching the gospel in areas where people had never heard of Jesus.

You may never go to unreached people groups in faraway lands, but it should still be your ambition to share the gospel with others. Part of your mission as a believer is to interact with others who don't know the love of God in Christ and to share it with them. People need to know the gospel—that God loves them so much that He sent His Son to die on the cross to provide a way for sinners to be reconciled to Him by faith. Those of us who have been impacted by the love of God in Christ should be eager to share it with those who do not follow Jesus.

At the present time, it is not very cool or trendy within the Church to be about sharing the gospel. The elevated talk these days is on ministries of mercy and justice. I am all-in for this ministry, as well, but we must not leave out gospel proclamation. We can physically help people all day long, but if we ignore their most pressing need—to be reconciled to a holy God, who stands against them and will not accept them apart from Christ—then we can't say we really love them. Because we care about the eternal destiny of humans, we want to make it our ambition to tell them about Jesus. And because we love them, we tell them that there is hope through the gospel. That is why we want the gospel to pervade our church and then move through us to the rest of the world.

That's what Paul was all about as he proclaimed the gospel and attempted to stir up the Church to do the same. The church that proclaims the gospel is a church made up of individuals who make it their ambition to share the gospel. Are you one of those individuals who makes this your ambition? In a grace-filled way, I say, YOU SHOULD BE. Every believer should be. Let me keep pressing you to action in sharing your faith by the power of the Holy Spirit. How about sharing the gospel with at least one person this week? Pray right now about who needs to hear about God's love for them in the gospel of Jesus Christ and pray for boldness to share with them. Whether you live among the reached or the unreached, make it your ambition to preach the gospel.

Memory Work

- Repeat 15 times Acts 1:8 and mark the back of the card each time you say it.
- Don't forget to say the reference before and after you say the verse.
- Return to Proverbs 4:23, 1 Corinthians 15:3–4, Ezekiel 36:27, 2 Timothy 3:16, and 1 John 4:7.
- Repeat each one time and mark the back of each card.

Day 24: Witness

Can you imagine being so passionate about something that it was your ambition to see it spread all over the world? Once, my wife and I met a woman with a global passion. We had a lengthy conversation with the first female employee of Facebook. Sheepishly, we told her that neither one of us were on Facebook and didn't plan to sign up any time soon. She was patient with us and even eager to articulate her passion for seeing Facebook benefit the whole world.

The goal she was particularly amped about was seeing Facebook hit one billion users around the world. We told her how we were overseas and met people who were connecting on Facebook and that it was happening in countries all over the world. Imagine how awesome that must be for her to see her passion, one she pours so much of her time and energy into, spread around the world. (Update: My wife is now on Facebook, but I'm still a holdout.)

Maybe you have a passion that you would love to see impact the world in some way. If you are in the medical or research field, then you might be encouraged if the advances that you have been a part of could impact the world. Perhaps you are a gifted musician or artist and would love to be a part of spreading your gifts into a variety of cultures. If you are a businessperson, you might like to promote work that enhances the common good in a variety of economies. But as wonderful as all those endeavors are, none of them compare to the one great passion that should unite all Christians: to leverage your life so that more and more people from all over the world become committed followers of Jesus. It should be an overriding zeal to go all-out in making disciples of the nations and taking part in what has been called the Great

Commission. No matter your vocation or calling in life, the Great Commission is the one unifying mission and passion for all believers, for all time.

Jesus sums up the Great Commission given to His disciples in Matthew 28:18–20:

> And Jesus came and said to them, "All authority in heaven and on earth has been given to me. Go therefore and make disciples of all nations, baptizing them in the name of the Father and of the Son and of the Holy Spirit, teaching them to observe all that I have commanded you. And behold, I am with you always, to the end of the age."

Jesus wants you to make disciples, which means He wants you to take part in leveraging your life so other people will follow Him. Just like His early disciples trusted, followed, obeyed, and worshiped Him, He wants you to invest in others so they will trust, follow, obey, and worship Jesus. And this is not something you go at alone or just with the Church, but Jesus Himself promises to be with you: "And behold, I am with you always, to the end of the age." He is not so much with you for comfort, but He is with you in the sense that He will see to it that, through the Church, His mission will go forward. His plan will ultimately succeed, as people from every tribe and language and nation will worship Jesus.

Go ahead and pursue your ambition and passion according to your unique gifting and calling, but the one overarching mission of making disciples is the one unifying ambition and passion for all believers. May you go all-out on Jesus' mission until He comes back in all His glory.

Memory Work

- Repeat 10 times Acts 1:8 and mark the back of the card each time you say it.
- Don't forget to say the reference before and after you say the verse.
- Return to Proverbs 4:23, 1 Corinthians 15:3–4, Ezekiel 36:27, 2 Timothy 3:16, and 1 John 4:7.
- Repeat each one time and mark the back of each card.

Compassion

Matthew 25:40

"And the King will answer them,
'Truly, I say to you,
as you did it to one of the least of
these my brothers, you did it to
me.'"

Day 25: Compassion

A few years back, my wife and I went to Jamaica. There are beautiful resorts all over the island, and although we did not have the privilege of staying at one of these places, I hear they are unbelievable. The food is all-you-can-eat pretty much all the time. The drinks are abundant. The rooms, the pools, and the beach accommodations are magnificent. The entertainment is top-notch, and the wait staff is ready at your service. Now, I am trying not to seem jealous or bitter because we lacked the resort setting, as we stayed outside of the luxurious resorts and experienced the heart of the Jamaican culture.

We saw the vast poverty and suffering. One day, we went to an orphanage and saw the abandoned and abused children who were dying for love and affection. We interacted with people who were poor and couldn't get jobs. We observed the drug culture, as I was offered drugs and drug paraphernalia. At the same time, it was a place permeated with the gospel and people who love Jesus. In the midst of the suffering, they are clinging to Christ. Nonetheless, there were plenty of opportunities for compassion.

Imagine if I had gone over to one of those fancy resorts and talked to the people there about what was going on outside the resort. I would have told them about the orphans who needed just the basic peanut butter and jelly to survive. Someone on the resort might have said, "But it's all-you-can-eat." I would have spoken about the danger and abuses that were happening to the vulnerable just a short distance away. Someone on the resort might have said, "But look at all the security guards." If I had told them how people were terribly sick and dying from the drug culture, which trickled down to the children in that society, someone on the resort might have said, "People look healthy." Then, what would have happened if I had said, "Look, let me get to the point? People are suffering, and they need your help. Would you please step off the resort and come and help them?"

The reality is that just about all of us, including myself, live on "the resort" every day. We have comfortable lives, and we live, for the most part, in prosperous surroundings. There is not much poverty, hunger, disease, or oppression going on where we live. This is nothing to feel guilty about; it is just the way it is. Yet, we are called as Christians to engage and help those who are in need, especially our brothers and sisters in the Lord.

However, in our normal day-to-day routines living on the resort, we will probably not bump up against such suffering. That is why I believe that our calling, in particular, is to step off the resort, to step out of our comfortable lives in order to show compassion to those who are suffering. It may be just down the street, or it may be around the world. The call to compassion in the Bible is clear that if we don't obey it, we don't know Jesus, and we will be judged for our actions. It is time to step off the resort.

Perhaps you have already stepped off the resort and are in the midst of caring for those who are suffering. Keep plowing ahead. Maybe you have the heart to show compassion, but you are not quite sure what to do. You really do love Jesus, but you have no outlet to show love to those who are suffering. Over the next few days, as you memorize God's Word about serving the "least of these," ask God to show you the part you play. May God stir you to compassion, so that you will step off the resort.

Memory Work

- Write out Matthew 25:40 along with the reference on the front of a 3x5 card.
- Write just the reference on the back of the card.
- Repeat it 25 times and mark the back of the card each time you say it.
- Say the reference before and after you say the verse.
- Return to Proverbs 4:23, 1 Corinthians 15:3–4, Ezekiel 36:27, 2 Timothy 3:16, 1 John 4:7, and Acts 1:8.
- Repeat each one time and mark the back of each card.

Day 26: Compassion

In a familiar passage, Jesus tells His disciples what it will be like at the final judgment. In Matthew 25:31–40, He says:

> "When the Son of Man comes in his glory, and all the angels with him, then he will sit on his glorious throne. Before him will be gathered all the nations, and he will separate people one from another as a shepherd separates the sheep from the goats. And he will place the sheep on his right, but the goats on the left. Then the King will say to those on his right, 'Come, you who are blessed by my Father, inherit the kingdom prepared for you from the foundation of the world. For I was hungry and you gave me food, I was thirsty and you gave me drink, I was a stranger and you welcomed me, I was naked and you clothed me, I was sick and you visited me, I was in prison and you came to me.' Then the righteous will answer him, saying, 'Lord, when did we see you hungry and feed you, or thirsty and give you drink? And when did we see you a stranger and welcome you, or naked and clothe you? And when did we see you sick or in prison and visit you?' And the King will answer them, 'Truly, I say to you, as you did it to

one of the least of these my brothers, you
did it to me.'"

You, along with the rest of humanity, will appear before the
judgment seat of Christ. The sheep will be placed on the right
side of favor, while on the left side will be the goats, who are to
face punishment in hell. This is not salvation based upon works,
because salvation is based upon faith in Jesus Christ alone. Yet,
true faith will always produce works. The separation of the sheep
and the goats is based upon those who had faith manifested in
compassionate works and those who had no faith at all. Jesus is
saying to those on His right, who are about to inherit the kingdom, that there were things done to Him by believers that were
a manifestation of their faith. When Jesus was in need, they
stepped up and met His need.

Jesus says, "As you did it to one of the least of these My
brothers, you did it to Me.'" What they have done for vulnerable Christians, they have done for Him. This passage is often
misinterpreted to mean that when you help the poor and
suffering, then you are help-ing Jesus. Yet, He is saying
that when you help *Christians* in need, you are indeed serving Jesus Himself, who is connected
with them. This doesn't mean that you shouldn't also help non-
Christians. Galatians 6:10 captures the idea well: "So then, as we
have opportunity, let us do good to everyone, and especially to
those who are of the household of faith." Yes, you should serve
and show compassion to non-Christians. But the emphasis here
is on how you associate and care for your fellow Christians in
need.

> . . . true faith will
> always produce
> works.

Jesus is saying that when they visited other believers who were
in jail, perhaps gospel messengers who were persecuted, then
they were visiting Him. Even today, prisons are difficult places,

but no matter the reason a believer (or unbeliever) is there, they are to be visited and shown compassion. In addition, when you give food and drink to the hungry and thirsty believers around the world, you are doing it to Jesus. When you visit sick and suffering Christians, you are visiting Jesus. You are not doing these things to earn salvation, but rather, because you already have a changed heart and love Jesus. If you love Jesus, you will love His people and all people. The evidence of faith is caring for those who are weak and lowly with gospel-produced compassion.

Memory Work

- Repeat 20 times Matthew 25:40 and mark the back of the card each time you say it.
- Don't forget to say the reference before and after you say the verse.
- Return to Proverbs 4:23, 1 Corinthians 15:3–4, Ezekiel 36:27, 2 Timothy 3:16, 1 John 4:7, and Acts 1:8.
- Repeat each one time and mark the back of each card.

Day 27: Compassion

As you are moved to have compassion on others, may it always be fueled by the compassion that the Lord Jesus has had on you. Divine compassion aimed at you empowers earthly compassion aimed at others. Consider the compassion of Jesus aimed at two blind men crying out for healing. Matthew 20:29–34 tells us:

> And as they went out of Jericho, a great crowd followed him. And behold, there were two blind men sitting by the roadside, and when they heard that Jesus was passing by, they cried out, "Lord, have mercy on us, Son of David!" The crowd rebuked them, telling them to be silent, but they cried out all the more, "Lord, have mercy on us, Son of David!" And stopping, Jesus called them and said, "What do you want me to do for you?" They said to him, "Lord, let our eyes be opened." And Jesus in pity touched their eyes, and immediately they recovered their sight and followed him.

The Son of David is filled with compassion. While Jesus was on this earth, He was filled with compassion for the suffering. You will find many instances in the Scriptures where Jesus was inwardly moved with compassion toward those who were lost and suffering.

Now, as the exalted Lord, He is still filled with compassion and ready to help you in your time of need. Hebrews 4:15–16 shares these comforting words:

> For we do not have a high priest who
> is unable to sympathize with our
> weaknesses, but one who in every respect
> has been tempted as we are, yet without
> sin. 16 Let us then with confidence draw
> near to the throne of grace, that we may
> receive mercy and find grace to help in
> time of need.

The Lord Jesus wants you to come to Him in your time of suffering, whether physical, emotional, or spiritual. You can keep going to the Lord over and over again.

At one point, I had to go to the Lord over and over again when my kids kept landing in the emergency room. In a short span, my middle daughter broke her arm, and then my oldest son injured his thumb. After that, my five-year-old son had two accidents that put us in the ER twice within twenty-four hours. On one occasion, he smashed his head against the wall and went to the ER to have his scalp glued back together. The next day, he smashed his forehead against a pole, and we were back in the same ER getting fifteen stiches. The Lord was just pouring His compassion on us over and over again as I cried out to Him.

In the midst of all the craziness, the Lord brought a little baby boy into our lives. He was within one mile of our house and had been through a lot of suffering. We didn't know what had happened to him or what was going to happen, but we knew that the compassion the Lord had been pouring out on us must now be poured out on this little child.

As you continue to go through the trials and sufferings of this life, don't forget that you must constantly go to the Lord for compassion, and His mercy and grace will overflow to help you in your time of need. But don't stop there. Ask the Lord for opportunities to let that same compassion overflow out of you onto others. May your compassion continue to be fueled by the compassion the Lord Jesus has shown to you.

Memory Work

- Repeat 15 times Matthew 25:40 and mark the back of the card each time you say it.
- Don't forget to say the reference before and after you say the verse.
- Return to Proverbs 4:23, 1 Corinthians 15:3–4, Ezekiel 36:27, 2 Timothy 3:16, 1 John 4:7, and Acts 1:8.
- Repeat each one time and mark the back of each card.

Day 28: Compassion

Deuteronomy 24:17–22 contains instructions for God's people to care for the most vulnerable, oppressed, and helpless in society: the sojourner, the fatherless, and the widow. Notice how the motivation to care for them springs from the fact that the Israelites themselves were once vulnerable, oppressed, and helpless as slaves in Egypt.

> You shall not pervert the justice due to the sojourner or to the fatherless, or take a widow's garment in pledge, but you shall remember that you were a slave in Egypt and the Lord your God redeemed you from there; therefore I command you to do this.
>
> When you reap your harvest in your field and forget a sheaf in the field, you shall not go back to get it. It shall be for the sojourner, the fatherless, and the widow, that the Lord your God may bless you in all the work of your hands. When you beat your olive trees, you shall not go over them again. It shall be for the sojourner, the fatherless, and the widow. When you gather the grapes of your vineyard, you shall not strip it afterward. It shall be for the sojourner, the fatherless, and the widow. You shall remember that you were a slave in the

land of Egypt; therefore I command you
to do this.

God has intervened to show compassion and rescue the vulnerable Israelites. Now they can show the same compassion and
love to others. To put it in Christian terms: The gospel motivates
compassion. Since you have been redeemed out of your spiritually vulnerable state of sin, you now move toward others who are
afflicted in their helpless condition.

When you think of the widow, the fatherless, and the sojourner, they tend to be people who are on posters, like the picture of
a starving child at your grocery checkout with a little donation
box next to it. You don't know that child, but if you feel pricked
enough in your heart, you will drop in some change and move on.

Let me make it a bit more personal. Let's say your mom is a
widow in a nursing home. After lying in her own filth for two
hours, she finally has someone to clean her up and take her to the
bathroom. But her caregiver is impatient with her slow movements and continues to knee her thighs over and over again, creating bruises. At night, she has visitors sneak into her room and
steal her stuff. What would you do for your mom?

Or, imagine that your own child is living in an orphanage in
a third world country, far away from you. Their stomach gnaws
in pain because there is not much food. Not a soul cares enough
to read to them or rock them to sleep. They have head lice and
a rash that causes them to itch all over. Their caretakers abuse
them emotionally, physically, and sometimes sexually. What
would you do for your child?

Say you live in another country, and you send your family
to America. You stay behind, but they show up in Chicago with
nothing. They are easy prey for people to take advantage of them
because they don't speak the language, know the culture, or have
any money or assets. What would you do for your family?

In all these situations you are emotionally connected. That's what God is doing here in Deuteronomy. He is reminding them that *that was their plight.* That was their condition as slaves in Egypt. They were to remember the conditions, and never forget. They were helpless, they were vulnerable, and they were oppressed. But not anymore; now they are redeemed. Since they have been an object of God's compassion and love, now they are to let His love and compassion spill out of them onto others.

Memory Work

- Repeat 10 times Matthew 25:40 and mark the back of the card each time you say it.
- Don't forget to say the reference before and after you say the verse.
- Return to Proverbs 4:23, 1 Corinthians 15:3–4, Ezekiel 36:27, 2 Timothy 3:16, 1 John 4:7, and Acts 1:8.
- Repeat each one time and mark the back of each card.

The Church

Hebrews 10:24-25

And let us consider how to stir up one another to love and good works, not neglecting to meet together, as is the habit of some, but encouraging one another, and all the more as you see the Day drawing near.

Day 29: The Church

Over the years, I have preached on Acts 2:42–47 more than any other passage. It's a great description of what the Church looks like in action. Acts 2 portrays the Day of Pentecost, when Peter preached the gospel of Jesus Christ to Jews from all around the world. About three thousand people repented of their sin and were baptized (Acts 2:41). The book of Acts starts out mentioning 120 believers (Acts 1:15), but now there are over three thousand. Talk about massive church growth and revival!

There are enough new believers to make up a small town. What happens next? It's laid out in Acts 2:42–47:

> And they devoted themselves to the
> apostles' teaching and the fellowship, to
> the breaking of bread and the prayers.
> And awe came upon every soul, and
> many wonders and signs were being
> done through the apostles. And all who
> believed were together and had all things
> in common. And they were selling
> their possessions and belongings and
> distributing the proceeds to all, as any
> had need. And day by day, attending the
> temple together and breaking bread in
> their homes, they received their food
> with glad and generous hearts, praising
> God and having favor with all the people.
> And the Lord added to their number day
> by day those who were being saved.

Even though this is a description of what happened in the early Church, it is clear from the rest of the New Testament that when God changes lives, it often looks like this. The way they lived as the Church was radical. At least it is radical to many in the Church today, but for them, it was just normal. Some of their practices might seem a bit extreme, but for them, it was normal. And I am hoping the normal of the early Church, which is often reserved for a few radical Christians, would become the *normal radical* for all in the modern Church.

> . . . what would you and your church look like if you lived the balanced normal-radical Christian life?

Do you want to live the normal-radical Christian life expressed in the early Church? Then it must be pursued with balance. You must strive for the balanced normal-radical Christian life.

Let me explain: In this passage, a variety of activities are often emphasized to the exclusion of others based on one's particular church tradition. Churches that are really into teaching doctrine will emphasize the apostolic teaching portion of the passage. Denominations that emphasize social justice will focus on the believers sharing their goods. Charismatics focus on the signs and wonders. Christian groups that are more communal in nature may emphasize the intimate fellowship. Movements that are more evangelistic and mission-minded love to emphasize all those who were being saved.

The late great Christian singer Rich Mullins said that as he traveled the world, he noticed that believers in different parts of the world underlined different parts of their Bibles. Mullins went on to say that if we put all the Bibles together in the world, then literally everything would be underlined.

It's great if you come from a certain background based on the Bible. The diversity of traditions is amazing. But what would you and your church look like if you lived the balanced normal-radical Christian life? Pray for yourself and your church to take all of these descriptions of the early Church in Acts 2 and live them out for the glory of God.

Memory Work

- Write out Hebrews 10:24–25 along with the reference on the front of a 3x5 card.
- Write just the reference on the back of the card.
- Repeat it 25 times and mark the back of the card each time you say it.
- Say the reference before and after you say the verse.
- Return to Proverbs 4:23, 1 Corinthians 15:3–4, Ezekiel 36:27, 2 Timothy 3:16, 1 John 4:7, Acts 1:8, and Matthew 25:40.
- Repeat each one time and mark the back of each card.

Day 30: The Church

L et's continue in Acts 2:42–47 and consider a couple of elements of the balanced normal-radical Christian life.

Apostolic Teaching: The apostles taught these new believers in biblical truth. The apostolic teaching was centered on Christ, all that He taught and did, along with the rest of the Bible that is fulfilled in Him. The core of this teaching has been handed down to you in the Bible. The apostolic teaching is the Word of God, and those who faithfully teach the Bible pass it on from one generation to the next.

Traditionally, the Protestant Reformation has emphasized the importance of the Word of God for every believer. Maybe you grew up in a church where the main emphasis was on preaching and teaching the Word of God. That's great! But even if you didn't, it's still crucial for you to be in a church full of people who are devoted to the Word of God, centered on Christ.

It is radical in our day and time to say you are devoted to God's Word. People may be fine if you are devoted to God, but for them, it's taking it too far when you also are devoted to His Word. Yet, God can't be separated from His Word, because in His Word, He reveals who He is.

> He calls for a response and obedience to who He is, and in our culture, that is considered radical.

He calls for a response and obedience to who He is, and in our culture, that is considered radical. Consider what God's Word says by Jesus' mouth in Luke 14:27: "Whoever does not bear his own cross and come after me cannot be my disciple." Jesus also says in Matthew 10:39: "Whoever finds his life will lose it, and whoever loses his life for my sake will find it." In God's Word, you see Jesus calling you to abandon your life for His sake, even to the point of death.

This sacrificial obedience is to impact all areas of your life. Many will say you are taking this religious stuff too far, and even so-called professing Christians will play down verses like this, possibly viewing you as an extremist. However, when you pick and choose what you want to keep or to leave out, you are playing God. You must accept the Word as it is and live it out, as it is written. Others may view you as a radical, but this is simply the radical-normal Christian life.

Prayer and Miracles: The early Church was a praying Church. They cried out to God with all types of thanksgiving and requests. They were asking God to move in mighty and powerful ways, and He did. All of these signs and wonders confirmed the apostles' teaching. There may be times, even today, where the miraculous occurs when the gospel is preached. The greatest power is seen in the conversion of sinners, but at times, the miraculous may be in healing or other powerful ways.

In our day and time, when I think about a group that emphasizes praying and the miraculous, it tends to be the charismatics. Maybe you come from a charismatic background, where you consistently pray for God to move in powerful and mighty ways. Wouldn't it be great if all Christians started to be more prayerful and expectant? Not expectant in the sense of an absolute guarantee, but practicing prayer with hopeful expectation, praying the type of prayer where you are not only praying for your daily routines but also asking for God to move in powerful ways. May the Lord stir you to be a part of a community that takes His Word seriously and prays expectantly, so that you are living out the normal-radical Christian life.

Memory Work

- Repeat 20 times Hebrews 10:24–25 and mark the back of the card each time you say it.
- Don't forget to say the reference before and after you say the verse.
- Return to Proverbs 4:23, 1 Corinthians 15:3–4, Ezekiel 36:27, 2 Timothy 3:16, 1 John 4:7, Acts 1:8, and Matthew 25:40.
- Repeat each one time and mark the back of each card.

Day 31: The Church

Let's stay with Acts 2:42–47 and consider a couple more elements of the balanced normal-radical Christian life.

Fulfillment of Needs: Acts 2:44 states: "And all who believed were together and had all things in common." You can't talk about how you are all in with community as long as you leave your money out of the conversation. The early Church was together, and in some sense, their money was put together and made available to those who had a need. Acts 2:45 goes on: "And they were selling their possessions and belongings and distributing the proceeds to all, as any had need." This wasn't mandatory, but an overflow of love. They saw people with a genuine need, and they responded in love. Later the passage says in Acts 4:34: "There was not a needy person among them ..." Can you imagine a church functioning to the point that they could say, "There will never be a needy person among us"?

> Whether you give through a program or not, personally invest in people.

In the past, there were strong movements that combined gospel preaching with care for the poor. The Salvation Army used to have a strong history of giving out the gospel and making provision for people physically. Maybe you come from a tradition where it is all about caring for those in need inside and outside the church. Maybe you make financial sacrifices so that your brothers and sisters can be cared for. In addition, you give your money away to those in need around the world. If you don't invest, perhaps it's not because you have a hard heart; maybe you just don't know where to start.

Let me encourage you to start by having a focus on personal investment. Whether you give through a program or not, personally invest in people. Invest in relationships and live a radical lifestyle of sacrificial giving.

Spread of the Gospel: Acts 2:46–47 describes the people's lifestyle: "And day by day, attending the temple together and breaking bread in their homes, they received their food with glad and generous hearts, praising God and having favor with all the people. And the Lord added to their number day by day those who were being saved."

As the early Church was meeting, worshiping, praying, and caring for one another, people were getting saved. The gospel was being preached, and God kept adding more and more people. God desires to add to His community, and He wants His people devoted to preaching the gospel. The Church is filled with historical movements that spread the gospel around the world.

Maybe you come from such a background. But how are you doing *now* with sharing the good news? Do you desire others to come to know Jesus and be reconciled to the Father? I'm not content or satisfied with where I am. I want this lack of gospel sharing to disturb you as it disturbs me. Out of love for God and a love for others, let's be aggressive in sharing our faith as individuals and together as church communities.

Memory Work

- Repeat 15 times Hebrews 10:24–25 and mark the back of the card each time you say it.
- Don't forget to say the reference before and after you say the verse.
- Return to Proverbs 4:23, 1 Corinthians 15:3–4, Ezekiel 36:27, 2 Timothy 3:16, 1 John 4:7, Acts 1:8, and Matthew 25:40.
- Repeat each one time and mark the back of each card.

Day 32: The Church

So far, you have seen the radical nature of the early Church in the way they received the Word, prayed expectantly, shared their faith, and cared for one another. None of this would be possible unless they were actually around one another. Notice what it says in Acts 2:42: "And they devoted themselves to ... the fellowship ..."

Fellowship is a biblical word—*koinonia*—and it means "participation." It refers to participation in one another's joys, sufferings, and hardships; participation in doing the work of the Lord together and a general sense of doing life together. Whether you come from a communal-living fellowship or not, fellowship should still be radical. Your fellowship and participation should go so far as even functioning as a family member. The body of Christ is your family. As natural families participate in life together, so is the case of your new spiritual family.

There are many people in the Church who can enter your life and offer you wisdom, direction, and love, maybe in a way you have never had before in your own family. My wife and I have experienced the fellowship of our local church, as many people have loved us, built into us, and lived life with us as we follow Jesus. No church is perfect, as no family is perfect, but fellowship within a local church should be the context for the normal-radical Christian life.

This is why it is crucial that you never stop meeting with a local body of believers. Hebrews 10:24–25 instructs, "And let us consider how to stir up one another to love and good works, not neglecting to meet together, as is the habit of some, but encouraging one another, and all the more as you see the Day drawing near." Maybe some of the Hebrews were afraid of being associated with the Church because of potential persecution coming their way. They pulled away from fellowship in fear and a lack of faith. Yet, they were to stay engaged in the fellowship, regardless of the circumstances, so they could be encouraged and encourage others as the Church waited for Jesus to return.

If you are inconsistent in gathering with the Church, what is your excuse? Most of the reasons given are lame. Why don't you just say, "I was functioning in unbelief like the Hebrews and thought it would be better for me to miss church"? Show me a Christian who is out of fellowship, and I'll show you a Christian who is struggling big-

> . . . it is crucial that you never stop meeting with a local body of believers.

time. You need the assembly of believers. You need the corporate worship and the preaching and teaching of God's Word. You need interpersonal interactions with others in small groups, Bible studies, and accountability. You need to be serving others with your gifts and your ministry. You are to be an integral part of the body of Christ. You are to be in the mix of encouraging others until Jesus comes back.

If you have been pulling away from the body of Christ for a while, take this time to repent, and ask God to help you to believe His Word—that you need the body of Christ, and they need you, as well. Let this passage sink into your heart once again: "And let us consider how to stir up one another to love and good works, not neglecting to meet together, as is the habit of some, but encouraging one another, and all the more as you see the Day drawing near."

Memory Work

- Repeat 10 times Hebrews 10:24–25 and mark the back of the card each time you say it.
- Don't forget to say the reference before and after you say the verse.
- Return to Proverbs 4:23, 1 Corinthians 15:3–4, Ezekiel 36:27, 2 Timothy 3:16, 1 John 4:7, Acts 1:8, and Matthew 25:40.
- Repeat each one time and mark the back of each card.

The Future

Proverbs 16:9

The heart of man plans his way,
but the Lord establishes his steps.

Day 33: The Future

People just out of high school, college, or graduate school are the ones who are often figuring out life and making future plans. But it's not as if you are finished planning when you knock out the big decisions of job, moving, and mate. It is amazing how people keep on planning for the future throughout all stages of their lives. Personal plans, work plans, and spiritual plans are just part of living, no matter your age. That's why it is important to grasp a biblical understanding of your future plans in light of God's plans. I want you to have a proper perspective of how your plans fit into God's plans.

Planning for the future is good, but it must be done with the appropriate heart. Proverbs 16:1 states:

> The plans of the heart belong to man,
> but the answer of the tongue is from the
> LORD.

The Bible is all for us making plans. The first part of Proverbs 21:5 says, "The plans of the diligent surely lead to abundance . . ." You have been created with a mind to work through different options. Your thoughts and motives make up your heart, which seeks to plan for the future. You have been given the ability to strategize and dream, and that's great— ". . . but the answer of the tongue is from the Lord." God's plan will be the ultimate outcome. The answer the person gives with the "tongue" is from the Lord. The idea is that a person makes plans, but the ultimate result will always be from the Lord. So, if you have been accepted to a school, your response will ultimately be what the Lord decrees in His sovereign will. If someone asks for your hand in marriage or you get a job offer, your response will be what God has decided in His providence. Your future plans are under the providence of God. God's sovereign will always makes the ultimate decision.

Be careful here: I want to make a distinction between God's moral will and His sovereign will. Many scholars use different language, but they come up with two distinctions concerning the will of God. God's *moral* will is His revealed will to us in the Word of God. It is His will that we obey His Word. But God's *sovereign* will is not known and is only seen as events unfold in life. The kind of planning I am talking about in this context has to do with your future planning in light of God's sovereign will, His controlling all outcomes, and His directing your life as He sees fit.

God has the final say about your future and your plans. Proverbs 16:9 says:

> The heart of a man plans his way,
> but the LORD establishes his steps.

You make plans, but the Lord determines what happens. No matter people's plans, they are not carried out unless they fit with God's. Proverbs 19:21 also makes this point clear:

> Many are the plans in the mind of a man,
> but it is the purpose of the LORD that will
> stand.

There are a lot of plans in the world today, and you even likely have all types of plans rattling around in your head, but only one plan will be carried out: God's. Every outcome is from the Lord. Let God's sovereign will give you peace that God is always going to be in control of your life. You can plan it all out, but at the same time, trust like crazy in God's perfect, sovereign will.

Memory Work

- Write out Proverbs 16:9 along with the reference on the front of a 3x5 card.
- Write just the reference on the back of the card.
- Repeat it 25 times and mark the back of the card each time you say it.
- Say the reference before and after you say the verse.
- Return to Proverbs 4:23, 1 Corinthians 15:3–4, Ezekiel 36:27, 2 Timothy 3:16, 1 John 4:7, Acts 1:8, Matthew 25:40, and Hebrews 10:24–25.
- Repeat each one time and mark the back of each card.

Day 34: The Future

As you think through your future plans, you should always be checking your heart motives. Proverbs 16:2 declares:

> All the ways of a man are pure in his own
> eyes, but the LORD weighs the spirit.

Most people believe their plans come from good motives. Maybe you assume that you are like the one in this proverb, whose plan is "pure in his own eyes." There may be times when you can't see how your plans could ever have less-than-pure motives. It's like you can trick and deceive yourself. Let's say you want a bigger house, and I ask you why. You say you want to host a small group, put up missionaries overnight, and have a big kitchen to feed all the homeless. Really? There are many plans that can seem "pure" in our own eyes.

'. . . But the LORD weighs the spirit." This statement emphasizes that the Lord knows your true motives. I see it as a ripping out of your heart—filled with your true motives and aspirations—so that everything is in the Lord's sight. This motive check by the Lord doesn't have to be known to you at death, but it can be known to you now. You can start to know your true motives in your plans. There are three ways you can start to know your true motives: through prayer, through the Word, and through others.

1. A good prayer is found in Psalm 139:23–24:

> Search me, O God, and know my heart!
> Try me and know my thoughts!

> And see if there be any grievous way in me,
> and lead me in the way everlasting!

2. The Word gets at our heart motives, as well. As Hebrews 4:12–13 explains:

> For the word of God is living and active,
> sharper than any two-edged sword,
> piercing to the division of soul and
> of spirit, of joints and of marrow, and
> discerning the thoughts and intentions of
> the heart. And no creature is hidden from
> his sight, but all are naked and exposed
> to the eyes of him to whom we must give
> account.

3. Brothers and sisters in the Lord are helpful for getting at your heart motives in your plans. You need counselors to protect you from yourself, as Proverbs 11:14 makes clear:

> Where there is no guidance, a people falls,
> but in an abundance of counselors there
> is safety.

The Lord has set these three safeguards to get at your heart, expose your motives, and bring you in line with Him. If you want to carry out your plans in a biblical way by praying, searching the Scriptures, and seeking the advice of others, there's a pretty good chance you will proceed with wisdom and good motives.

I am a dreamer, always coming up with crazy ideas, and my motives are often all over the place. Sometimes I can pray about a situation and ask the Lord to search me, but I am not as sensitive to the Holy Spirit's conviction as I should be. I can even read the Word and think the Scripture doesn't really apply to me. But it's really hard to get past that last safeguard of other people who speak truth into my life.

What's going on in your heart motives today with regard to your future? Ask the Lord to search your heart, diligently search the Scriptures, and reach out to your brothers and sisters for guidance.

Memory Work

- Repeat 20 times Proverbs 16:9 and mark the back of the card each time you say it.
- Don't forget to say the reference before and after you say the verse
- Return to Proverbs 4:23, 1 Corinthians 15:3–4, Ezekiel 36:27, 2 Timothy 3:16, 1 John 4:7, Acts 1:8, Matthew 25:40, and Hebrews 10:24–25.
- Repeat each one time and mark the back of each card.

Day 35: The Future

L et's say you have the right perspective on your future plans and even good motives. Now it's time for commitments. Proverbs 16:3 instructs us to:

> Commit your work to the LORD,
> and your plans will be established.

This means a handing over all of it to the Lord. The word *commit* literally means "to roll." I picture the rolling of a big rock: You have your big rock of plans, full of details, and your accompanying motives, and you roll them into the presence of God. You roll them in with a sense of humility and hopefulness, and you are relaxed and at peace in God's sovereign control. You roll them in with prayer to check your motives, with His Word to expose your heart, and with the counsel of others to protect you from yourself. You roll all these plans before God and let Him decide what is to happen. Or, as one of my professors has said, you take all your plans before God—and you leave them there.

"...And your plans will be established." If God agrees with the plans in His sovereign decree, they will be established and come to fruition, but you have to leave the results to God. Sometimes things don't go as planned, even if you have good plans and good motives. Sometimes God has an even greater plan than what you had in mind. Your job is to plan, pray, seek counsel, roll it into God's presence, and trust Him for the outcome.

At times, you may be disappointed or confused that your future plans didn't work out as you wanted, but God is still in control. The prophet felt this, as he said in Jeremiah 10:23:

> I know, O LORD, that the way of man is
> not in himself, that it is not in man who
> walks to direct his steps.

Proverbs 20:24 adds:

> A man's steps are from the LORD;
> how then can man understand his way?

You don't know all the factors involved in your life or your future. But God is sovereign, and He is in absolute control along every step of the way. You can't figure it all out, but you must trust the Lord, who directs your journey through life. You trust Him by obeying His revealed will and by planning, while at the same time believing His sovereign plans are perfect. Often, you can look back and say, "God, You totally knew what You were doing. I praise You for directing me all along." Now as you move forward, you can trust in God and His ultimate plan for your life.

My favorite verse in the Bible is found in Ephesians 1:11 (NIV): "In him we were also chosen, having been predestined according to the plan of him who works out everything in conformity with the purpose of his will." God's plan was to save you in Christ. His plan was to send Jesus as your Savior, who died and rose again. Now, through repentance and faith, you can have eternal life. What a great plan. You should rejoice in God's gospel plan! But God also "works out everything in conformity with the purpose of his will." The same God who planned your salvation also ordains all the details in your life. He is working out His purposes in your life and plans. As you plan for the future, you plan as one who, in Christ, has been brought into God's plan. So now, in God's great plan, you can step into the future as one who is humble, hopeful, and peaceful in Christ.

Memory Work

- Repeat 15 times Proverbs 16:9 and mark the back of the card each time you say it.
- Don't forget to say the reference before and after you say the verse
- Return to Proverbs 4:23, 1 Corinthians 15:3–4, Ezekiel 36:27, 2 Timothy 3:16, 1 John 4:7, Acts 1:8, Matthew 25:40, and Hebrews 10:24–25.
- Repeat each one time and mark the back of each card.

Day 36: The Future

As you think about your future, I want to give you two images I keep coming back to as I encourage others and myself:

The first one has to do with planning your career or calling in life. You must plan what you major in, plan your job search, plan your career shifts, plan your future, and plan a variety of other parts of your vocational life. Part of planning is understanding yourself. It's very important to understand your abilities, passions, and gifts.

What do you do well? What do you enjoy? What is in your gift zone? It is very important to plan and live within your zone of gift-mix and ability. Dave Kraft explains the concept of Comfort Zone versus Gift Zone versus Danger Zone. Kraft says, "We should be open to the *challenge* of moving out of our "comfort zone," but *careful* about moving out of our "gift zone" into the "danger zone."[2] You need to stretch yourself beyond your comfort zone and grow and take risks that stretch you. But be careful, or you may fall out of your gift zone and enter the danger zone. This is where you become driven and overreaching.

Perhaps you have a great job where you are around people all the time, and you are being challenged in your gift zone. But there is another job you could get that would put you by yourself most of the time. You'd be crunching numbers, which isn't your thing at all and would only wear you out. The money is great and

---

2. Dave Kraft blog, Leadership From the Heart, "Staying in Your Gift Zone, but Getting Out of Your Comfort Zone," 2/19/2015. https://davekraft .org/2015/02/19/staying-in-your-gift-zone-but-getting-out-of-your-comfort -zone/.

tempting, but you need to watch out for the danger zone. As you plan in your heart, remember to know yourself, your gifts, and your passions. Try to stay within who God created you to be as you make your future plans.

The second image has to do with your desire to predict how all the details of your future will turn out. You know how high-definition video is so clear and beautiful? You want to see your career transitions, your relationship shifts, your advancements, and setbacks, and you want to see all the way into in retirement—in HD.

Yet, that is not the way it works, because God is God, and you are not.

Your future in the Lord is less like HD and more like a Polaroid picture. This description of a Polaroid picture has been out there for a while. I first learned it at a conference on "Calling" from Peter Richardson, and I have used it ever since. Your future, rather than being as clear as HD, is more like the slow exposure of a Polaroid picture—from opaque to hazy and to the final result. It's not clear up-front, and if you are waiting for absolute clarity before you do anything, you will be waiting a long time. God's calling for your life develops slowly as you step out and live in full dependence on Him. I believe God has set it up this way so that you would enjoy a relationship with Him, so that each day you would get up and seek the face of God for wisdom and direction, so that each day you would ask God for wisdom in planning and working hard while trusting in His sovereign control. Each day you must ask God to search your heart. Each day you must totally commit your life transitions to Him while leaving the results in His hands. May you seek Him today and trust Him to expose His plan for your life until you see Him face-to-face.

Memory Work

- Repeat 10 times Proverbs 16:9 and mark the back of the card each time you say it.
- Don't forget to say the reference before and after you say the verse
- Return to Proverbs 4:23, 1 Corinthians 15:3–4, Ezekiel 36:27, 2 Timothy 3:16, 1 John 4:7, Acts 1:8, Matthew 25:40, and Hebrews 10:24–25.
- Repeat each one time and mark the back of each card.

Glory

Romans 8:18

For I consider that the sufferings of this present time are not worth comparing with the glory that is to be revealed to us.

Day 37: Glory

The apostle Paul is so assured of the future glory that his present sufferings don't even enter into the realm of comparison. In light of eternal glory with God, suffering is just a blip on the screen. He says something similar in 2 Corinthians 4:17: "For this light momentary affliction is preparing for us an eternal weight of glory beyond all comparison." I once printed out this verse in a really large font and then went into a nursing home room of an elderly lady named Mrs. O'Neal. She was a lady who suffered greatly in the body, but she loved the Lord. She was sleeping, so I stuck it right on her body so she would see it when she woke up. It is encouraging that this temporary suffering is light and momentary while glory is weighty and eternal. Paul is not diminishing suffering, because sin has tainted everything in this world, including creation, yet even creation is looking forward to this liberation.

Romans 8:19–21 tell us:

> For the creation waits with eager longing for the revealing of the sons of God. For the creation was subjected to futility, not willingly, but because of him who subjected it, in hope that the creation itself will be set free from its bondage to corruption and obtain the freedom of the glory of the children of God.

The imagery here is of the creation longing for us to be free from the presence of sin and with the Lord forever in resurrected bodies. This future hope for us is also a future hope for creation.

Due to Adam and Eve's fall into sin, the creation became cursed by God (Gen. 3:17–19). Yet, the time will come when believers will be glorified and creation will be transformed into a new heaven and a new earth (Revelation 21:1–22:5).

While the creation waits for freedom, it groans in verse 22: "For we know that the whole creation has been groaning together in the pains of childbirth until now." Not only is the creation groaning, but believers do, as well. Verse 23 goes on: "And not only the creation, but we ourselves, who have the firstfruits of the Spirit, groan inwardly as we wait eagerly for adoption as sons, the redemption of our bodies." Here, you get a fuller picture of what is meant by glory. Not only is it the new heaven and the new earth, but it is also "the redemption of our bodies."

> . . . the time will come when believers will be glorified and creation will be transformed into a new heaven and a new earth (Revelation 21:1–22:5).

When believers die, their souls go to be with the Lord, but their bodies remain on this earth. At the second coming of Christ, their bodies are united with their souls, and they are glorified with the Lord forever. This, in a sense, is the completion of our adoption as sons. Believers eagerly look forward to that time and know it will happen because they have the "firstfruits of the Spirit." Just as a farmer has the first batch of his crop with the promise of more to come, so believers have the fullness of the Holy Spirit, which is a pledge of what is to come in the redemption of their bodies in glory.

For now, you do a double "groan." You groan in suffering and you groan with longing. You suffer now with persecutions, physical pain (sickness, barrenness, chronic pain), relational pain (conflicts, prodigal children, troubles with coworkers), and the struggle with sin (addictions). While you groan with longing, you push forward to live in the fullness of your adoption with the Lord forever. Keep pressing on in your groaning, for your longing will soon be fulfilled, as you will be with the Lord forever.

Memory Work

- Write out Romans 8:18 along with the reference on the front of a 3x5 card.
- Write just the reference on the back of the card.
- Repeat it 25 times and mark the back of the card each time you say it.
- Say the reference before and after you say the verse.
- Return to Proverbs 4:23, 1 Corinthians 15:3–4, Ezekiel 36:27, 2 Timothy 3:16, 1 John 4:7, Acts 1:8, Matthew 25:40, Hebrews 10:24–25, and Proverbs 16:9.
- Repeat each one time and mark the back of each card.

Day 38: Glory

Let me tell you an old wedding story. Once upon a time, a man and a woman were to get married. Now, the bride had ten bridesmaids; some were wise, and some were a bit foolish. Part of the tradition during this time was for the bridesmaids to leave the bride, then go out and meet the groom along with his entourage of friends and family. Then, they would accompany him in a huge processional to the wedding feast. This took place at night, so each bridesmaid had her own oil lamp, which was more like a torch. Five of the ten bridesmaids brought extra oil. The wise ones wanted to be prepared in case of a delay, but the foolish ones didn't really care.

Well, what do you know? The bridegroom was delayed, and all ten of these girls fell asleep out in the dark while waiting for the wedding party. All of a sudden, around midnight, they heard a cry: "Here is the bridegroom! Come out to meet him." They all woke up and tried to get their lamps going again. But the foolish ones didn't have any extra oil, so they asked the wise ones for oil. The wise ones said that there was not enough for both, so they should go to the twenty-four-hour oil supply dealership to buy their own.

So, the foolish bridesmaids took off for the dealership to get more oil, but while they were gone, the bridegroom came. The five ready bridesmaids went into the marriage feast with the bridegroom, and the door to the feast was shut. Then, the five foolish ones who finally got oil in their lamps came back to the feast. They noticed the door was shut, so they went up to the door and said, "Lord, lord, open to us." The reply came back, "Truly, I say to you, I do not know you." The End.

What kind of wedding story is that? This was a story told by Jesus to His disciples in Matthew 25:1–12. The main point of the story was that Jesus is coming back, like the bridegroom. He could return to earth at any time, and the disciples, like the wise bridesmaids, must be ready. Right after He told the story, He said, in Matthew 25:13, "Watch therefore, for you know neither the day nor the hour." To *watch* is to be constantly vigilant and ready for the return of Jesus Christ. Are you prepared for Jesus' return? Are you ready to meet Him right now?

What does it mean to be *ready*? Essentially, it means following Jesus and living a life of obedience while you long for His return. For example, Titus 2:11–14 tells us:

> For the grace of God has appeared,
> bringing salvation for all people, training
> us to renounce ungodliness and worldly
> passions, and to live self-controlled,
> upright, and godly lives in the present
> age, [Paul doesn't stop there, but speaks
> of a future grace to come] waiting for
> our blessed hope, the appearing of the
> glory of our great God and Savior Jesus
> Christ, who gave himself for us to redeem
> us from all lawlessness and to purify for
> himself a people for his own possession
> who are zealous for good works.

You are saved by grace through faith in Christ, which leads to holiness. As you await the return of Christ, you want to live a holy life and be spiritually awake at His return, where you will receive more grace and be set free from the struggle forever. Come, Lord Jesus!

Memory Work

- Repeat 20 times Romans 8:18 and mark the back of the card each time you say it.
- Don't forget to say the reference before and after you say the verse.
- Return to Proverbs 4:23, 1 Corinthians 15:3–4, Ezekiel 36:27, 2 Timothy 3:16, 1 John 4:7, Acts 1:8, Matthew 25:40, Hebrews 10:24–25, and Proverbs 16:9.
- Repeat each one time and mark the back of each card.

Day 39: Glory

The reality of Christ's return should revitalize you spiritually. The One whom you love and worship is coming back, which should impact the way you live right now. You must keep His return before your eyes and be changed on a deep level. He is coming to bring you out of this place of sin to a place of perfect righteousness, where you will live with Him forever in glory. Consider the words in 2 Peter 3:10–13:

> The One whom you love and worship is coming back, which should impact the way you live right now.

> But the day of the Lord will come like a thief, and then the heavens will pass away with a roar, and the heavenly bodies will be burned up and dissolved, and the earth and the works that are done on it will be exposed.

> Since all these things are thus to be dissolved, what sort of people ought you to be in lives of holiness and godliness, waiting for and hastening the coming of the day of God, because of which the heavens will be set on fire and dissolved, and the heavenly bodies will melt as they burn! But according to his promise we are

> waiting for new heavens and a new earth
> in which righteousness dwells.

Peter says, ". . . What sort of people ought you to be in lives of holiness and godliness . . . !" His expression shows that it is a no-brainer conclusion. If Jesus is coming back and the world is to be judged, you must live a holy life, separate from the sin of this world. The apostle Paul gives us some good categories in Colossians 3 to think through, things you should both avoid and pursue. You need to get rid of and put to death "sexual immorality, impurity, passion, evil desire, and covetousness . . . anger, wrath, malice, slander, and obscene talk" (vv. 5 and 8). The things you should pursue connected with your new home are "compassionate hearts, kindness, humility, meekness, and patience, bearing with one another, . . . forgiving each other. . . . And above all these put on love" (vv. 12–14). So, you separate yourself from the world of sin and pursue a life connected with the world to come in glory.

You are not just separating from your sin because of the coming judgment, but also because of your future home. Second Peter 3:13 says: "But according to his promise we are waiting for new heavens and a new earth in which righteousness dwells." Believers are looking forward to the promise of a "new heavens and a new earth in which righteousness dwells." Righteousness dwells there because God is there. And this place is reserved only for those transformed by the gospel.

Those in this life who realize they are sinners saved by the grace of God through faith in Jesus will enter the new heavens and the new earth. You are to wait and long for this future of righteousness where you will be delivered from your struggle with sin and come into an existence of perfect righteousness with God and with others. You will actually live a holy life and treat one another perfectly all the time. This vision of a promised future is to capture your heart now and spur you on to holiness.

Since you are waiting for this promise, you live a life of holiness and godliness now.

Second Peter 3:14 states: "Therefore, beloved, since you are waiting for these, be diligent to be found by him without spot or blemish, and at peace." Since you are literally waiting for the coming of Christ, the judgment of God, and the establishment of the new heavens and a new earth, you are not to be idle, but diligent. You shouldn't wait passively, but actively. You intentionally want to make sure you are in Christ, living a life of holiness without spot or blemish and at peace with God. This is not about working for your salvation, but working out your salvation, which continues even today.

Memory Work

- Repeat 15 times Romans 8:18 and mark the back of the card each time you say it.
- Don't forget to say the reference before and after you say the verse.
- Return to Proverbs 4:23, 1 Corinthians 15:3–4, Ezekiel 36:27, 2 Timothy 3:16, 1 John 4:7, Acts 1:8, Matthew 25:40, Hebrews 10:24–25, and Proverbs 16:9.
- Repeat each one time and mark the back of each card.

Day 40: Glory

Jude 24–25 provides this beautiful benediction: "Now to him who is able to keep you from stumbling and to present you blameless before the presence of his glory with great joy, to the only God, our Savior, through Jesus Christ our Lord, be glory, majesty, dominion, and authority, before all time and now and forever. Amen."

You may have previously heard this doxology at the end of church services. The original context is that of a church under attack from false teachers who were promoting false living. In this perilous situation, Jude encourages the Church to contend for the faith. They were to strive and fight against false teaching. Not only were they to be on the alert against false teaching, but they were also to keep themselves in God's love by growing in Jesus, praying in the Spirit, and waiting for His return.

Securely in Christ, they were to have mercy on drifting peers by snatching them from the fire. But through it all, God was holding on to them and keeping them in His persevering love until the day of Christ Jesus. The doxology that gives glory to God reminds them of God's all powerful, preserving authority to keep them forever. Jude ends his emphasis on contending for the faith on a note of rest. This doxology is the believers' rest as they place themselves in the hands of the all-powerful, sovereign God, who will keep them forever.

Verse 24 says: "Now to Him who is able to keep you from stumbling . . ." *Stumbling* has the idea of falling and being lost forever in hell. Jude was giving glory to God in His persevering power, but that blessing would come back down to believers, who are reminded that God will keep them from falling away. Not that you won't ever sin, but you won't stray so far as to love your sin enough to refuse repentance, deny the faith, and be lost. If you are a child of God and are truly saved, He will hold on to you and guard you against falling away. God's persevering love does not contradict the warnings throughout Jude, nor even the command to "keep yourselves in the love of God." Those commands are part of God's means to keep believers in His love. But the bottom line is this: You can rest in the One who keeps and guards you by His grace.

Verse 24 goes on to say: ". . . and [He will] present you blameless before the presence of his glory with great joy." God will keep and guard you against stumbling and will one day present you blameless in His presence. *Blameless* has the idea of being without blemish. In the Old Testament, a sacrificial lamb was to be offered to God without blemish or defect as an atoning sacrifice for the people's sins. It was an image that ultimately pointed to Jesus, who was the Lamb of God, without the blemish or defect of sin, who died in place of sinners. Those who put their faith in Christ will one day be presented blameless before God, not because we are perfect, but because of the righteousness of Christ. You will be accepted in God's presence because of the spotless One, Jesus Christ, and through His life, death, and resurrection. You can rest in God's finished work in Christ, who will present us "blameless" in the presence of His glory.

Verse 25 continues: "To the only God, our Savior, through Jesus Christ our Lord, be glory, majesty, dominion, and authority, before all time and now and forever. Amen." We find rest in the everlasting sovereign God, both now and forevermore. Amen.

Memory Work

- Repeat 10 times Romans 8:18 and mark the back of the card each time you say it.
- Don't forget to say the reference before and after you say the verse.
- Return to Proverbs 4:23, 1 Corinthians 15:3–4, Ezekiel 36:27, 2 Timothy 3:16, 1 John 4:7, Acts 1:8, Matthew 25:40, Hebrews 10:24–25, and Proverbs 16:9.
- Repeat each one time and mark the back of each card.

Afterword

Keep going! Add your own favorite verses or check out the app, which contains a fresh set for forty more days. Make Scripture memory a lifetime habit and joy!

About the Author

Jason Lancaster, Th.M. (Dallas Theological Seminary), D.Min. (Trinity Evangelical Divinity School), has spent the last twenty-plus years pastoring churches in the Los Angeles (Providence Church) and Chicago (Evanston Bible Fellowship) areas, helping the younger generation to launch out in life. Now he ministers in a retirement community in Hot Springs Village, Arkansas (Village Bible Church), helping people to land in life. Jason is married with seven children who are all adjusting from city life to farm life.

All royalties are given to support The Call, whose goal is to mobilize the church in Arkansas to love foster children with the extravagant love of Christ through fostering and adoption. Check them out at www.thecallinarkansas.org.